LEGENDS OF WARFARE

GROUND

Sherman Tank, Vol. 4

The M4A3 Medium Tank in World War II and Korea

DAVID DOYLE

SCHIFFER MILITARY

4880 Lower Valley Road   Atglen, PA 19310

Designed by Justin Watkinson
Type set in Impact/Minion Pro/Univers LT Std

ISBN: 978-0-7643-6142-5
Printed in China

Published by Schiffer Publishing, Ltd.
4880 Lower Valley Road
Atglen, PA 19310
Phone: (610) 593-1777; Fax: (610) 593-2002
E-mail: Info@schifferbooks.com
www.schifferbooks.com

For our complete selection of fine books on this and related subjects, please visit our website at www.schifferbooks.com.
You may also write for a free catalog.

Schiffer Publishing's titles are available at special discounts for bulk purchases for sales promotions or premiums. Special editions, including personalized covers, corporate imprints, and excerpts, can be created in large quantities for special needs. For more information, contact the publisher.

We are always looking for people to write books on new and related subjects. If you have an idea for a book, please contact us at proposals@schifferbooks.com.

Acknowledgments

This book would not have been possible without the gracious help of many individuals and institutions. This book would not have been possible without the gracious help of many individuals and institutions. Beyond the invaluable help provided by the staffs of Fiat-Chrysler North America, the TACOM LCMC History Office, the National Archives, and the Patton Museum, I am deeply indebted to Tom Kailbourn, Scott Taylor, Rob Ervin, Richard Hunnicutt, Mike Haines, Dana Bell, Don Moriarty, Chun Hsu, Chris Hughes, Joe DeMarco, Kurt Laughlin, and Pat Stansell. Their generous and skillful assistance adds immensely to the quality of this volume. In addition to such wonderful friends and colleagues, the Lord has blessed me with a wonderful wife, Denise, who has tirelessly scanned thousands of photos and documents for this and numerous other books. Beyond that, she is an ongoing source of support and inspiration.

Contents

Introduction

The M4 Sherman series of medium tanks not only formed the backbone of the US armored force during World War II but filled the ranks both of US and Allied nations' armies in the immediate post–World War II era as well. With a cumulative output of nearly 50,000 units, the Sherman was the Western Allies' most widely produced tank during World War II and far exceeded Germany's entire tank production from 1939 to 1945.

The origins of the M4 series of tanks can be traced to the changing world situation, especially in Europe, in the late 1930s. These factors led the US Army Ordnance Department to issue a contract in August 1940 for the production of 1,000 M2A1 medium tanks. To manufacture these tanks, Chrysler was contracted to operate the to-be-constructed Detroit Arsenal Tank Plant. However, German armored victories against a variety of nations proved that the M2A1 was obsolete before the plant would be finished. As a result, Rock Island Arsenal constructed the few M2A1s that were actually built (which were subsequently used as training tanks), and the new Detroit plant instead would produce the M3 medium tank, itself an interim vehicle. The "General Lee," as the M3 would come to be known, while an improvement over the M2A1, had many shortcomings. Most notably, its 75 mm gun was mounted in a sponson with limited traverse. The secondary weapon, a 37 mm antitank gun, was mounted in a turret with 360-degree rotation.

By February 1941, the problem of turret-mounting the 75 mm gun seemed to have been solved, and as a result a mockup of a new medium-tank design had begun to take shape at Aberdeen Proving Ground. Designated the T6, the new tank would utilize the lower hull, suspension, and drivetrain of the M3. A new, cast-armor hull and cast turret would be used. The turret would have a ring of 69 inches and a removable front plate to allow easy removal of the 75 mm main gun. By September 1941, an operational pilot of the T6 had been assembled at Aberdeen. Interestingly, this was only six months after the M3 pilot had been completed.

The T6 quickly evolved into the M4 Sherman, powered by a radial engine of Wright design but produced by Continental. The engine was essentially an aircraft engine, and demands for aircraft engines were such that the medium-tank program faced a serious engine shortage. Beginning with the M3, various other power plants were installed, including the GM 6046 diesel and the Chrysler Multibank.

A solution presented itself through the adaptation of another aircraft engine. Ford Motor Company had been working on a V-12 aircraft engine, which while not used for its intended purpose was instead cut down to a V-8, becoming the GAA tank engine. This engine was used to power the M4A3, the Sherman variant that is the subject of this volume, and it quickly became the favorite of the US Army.

The M3 Lee series of tanks were the direct ancestor of the M4 Sherman family of vehicles. While the M3 suffered from a sponson-mounted main gun, production of these vehicles paved the way for the Sherman. The M3 power train design and many other components were taken into the Sherman, and the mass-production techniques honed through the production of the Lee were invaluable in Sherman production. Among those was the welding method for armored-hull production, introduced on the M3A2 (*shown here*) and used in the production of the M4A3. *Patton Museum*

The prototype for the Medium Tank M4 family was the Medium Tank T6, which used the same hull, drivetrain, and engine as the Medium Tank M3. Construction of the T6 began in the summer of 1941, and it was rolled out on September 3, 1941. The vehicle featured a fully rotating turret with room for three crewmen. The main armament was a 75 mm Gun M2, equipped with a counterweight on the muzzle end to compensate for the short barrel until the longer-barreled 75 mm Gun M3 became available. An armored door was mounted on each sponson; no hatch door was provided for the assistant driver. *Ordnance Museum*

The first production Sherman was the Medium Tank M4A1, which had a cast upper hull with no side doors. The example shown here was transferred to the British and is seen here on display in London with a placard on the sponson that reads "MICHAEL," a tribute to Michael Dewar, chief of the British Tank Mission. The main gun remained the 75 mm Gun M2, with a counterweight on the barrel. In addition to the flexible bow machine gun, two fixed .30-caliber machine guns were mounted at the center of the glacis. *Patton Museum*

From the outset the M4 series of vehicles were planned to be powered by the R-975 Continental radial engine (*right rear*). As was the case during M3 production, demand outstripped the supply of these engines, leading some tanks to be powered by the GM 6046 twin diesel (*right foreground*), M3A3, M4A2 or the Chrysler Multibank (*left foreground*), M3A4, or M4A4. However, the Ford GAA V-8, which was introduced with the M4A3, quickly became the favorite of the US Army. *FCA North America Archives*

CHAPTER 1
M4A3 Small-Hatch, Dry-Stowage Tanks

Since there was a scarcity of Continental radial power plants, the Armored Board had to seek out other sources for the tank engines that existing plants could produce. The GAA V-8 gasoline engine made by Ford was a relatively compact modification of a 500-horsepower, V-12 experimental aircraft power plant. The Sherman's engine compartment, originally designed for tall radial engines, readily accommodated the Ford GAA. Modifications to facilitate installation of the Ford power plant eventually resulted in the M4A3. Under two production orders, all small-hatch (dry-stowage) M4A3 tanks were built by Ford Motor Company at that firm's Highland Park, Michigan, facility, located on the outskirts of Detroit.

The glacis on early production models included direct-vision ports. T-3034, the first production order, included 350 tanks and ran from June 1942 through January 1943. Another 1,340 tanks were manufactured under the second production order, T-3334, which lasted from November 1942 through September 1943. None of these small-hatch vehicles served in combat in their as-built configuration. Nearly all of them were used as training tanks for US forces, though some were subsequently remanufactured and improved and then posted to combat duty.

The first model of the Medium Tank M4A3 was a small-hatch, dry-stowage version, produced by Ford Motor Company at its factory in Highland Park, Michigan. Internally, the M4A3 was distinguished from other Sherman tanks by its Ford GAA V-8 engine. Externally, this tank varied from other models of the Sherman by the layout of its engine deck and sponson tops and the design of the rear of its hull. Here, Ford's pilot M4A3 is being rolled out on May 13, 1943. *Benson Ford Archives*

The glacis of the pilot M4A3 had a wide, rounded ridge to the left of the bow machine gun that was similar to those on early-production American Locomotive and Pullman-Standard M4A2s. This ridge was associated with a twin machine-gun mount originally to have been installed in these hulls. The driver and the assistant driver were provided with direct-vision ports with hinged, armored covers. Above these ports are the drivers' small-hatch doors. *Benson Ford Archives*

A new M4A3 leaves the Ford Highland Park plant on June 4, 1942. The main armament was the 75 mm Gun M4 on the Combination Gun Mount M34. That mount included an armored shield that was screwed to, and was mounted flush with, the turret face. On the front of the gun shield was a rotor shield, or mantlet, which early on, as seen here, was narrow, leaving much of the gun shield exposed. *Benson Ford Archives*

Marked with the number "6" on the glacis, a Ford small-hatch M4A3 is undergoing a test run on June 23, 1942. On the gun shield above the driver's head is the elongated port for the Browning M1919A4 .30-caliber coaxial machine gun. Protruding from the right side of the roof of the turret is an early-type vane sight, which the vehicle commander used to roughly align the 75 mm gun on a target. *Benson Ford Archives*

This series of photos of the Ford-built pilot M4A3 was taken during evaluations of the vehicle by the Ordnance Operation, General Motors Proving Ground, on May 29, 1942. Both direct-vision port covers are open. The drum-shaped extension atop the antenna bracket on the right side of the glacis was not carried over to production M4A3s. The forward lifting eyes had continuous pads on the bottom, which were welded to the glacis. *Patton Museum*

When the Ford pilot M4A3 was rolled out of the factory on May 13, 1942, it had the D37892 bogie assemblies, also called the initial-type suspension, with bogie assemblies similar to those of the Medium Tank M3, with the track-support roller centered above the bogie bracket. By the time these photos of the pilot M4A3 were taken on May 29, the original bogies were replaced by D47527 bogie assemblies, with the rollers mounted on arms to the upper rear and with steel skids installed on the tops of the bogie bracket. For some unexplained reason, the rear bogie was oriented with the roller to the front. The slope of the glacis of the small-hatch M4A3, 57 degrees from vertical, is displayed. *Patton Museum*

The two grille/doors on the engine deck of the pilot M4A3 were not similar to the design of the doors of the production M4A3s. The pilot's grilles constituted a T shape, while the two doors of the production tanks formed a rectangle that spanned the whole deck, excepting the sponsons. Also available for study are the shapes of the drivers' hoods and hatches, with rotating periscope mounts; the locations of the ventilators to the sides of those hatches, on the turret roof and to the left of the turret bustle; the locations of the loader's (*left*) and gunner's (*right*) periscopes on the turret roof; and the design of the turret hatch, with its split doors, one of which had a rotating periscope, and a mount for a machine gun on the hatch ring. *Patton Museum*

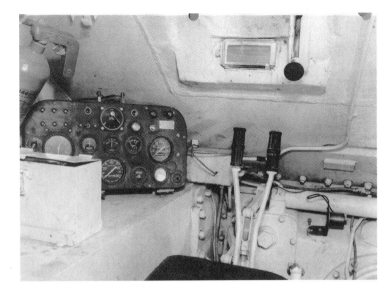

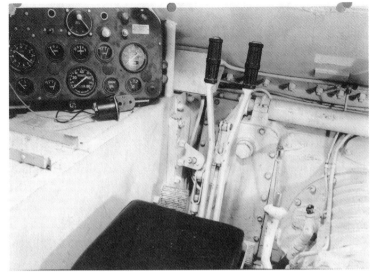

In the driver's station of the Ford pilot M4A3, at the top is the direct-vision port, to the left of which is the operating lever for the armored cover of the port. Below the port are the steering-brake control levers. To the front of the right lever is the cover for the left steering brake, with the hex-shaped cap for the brake adjustment near the top. To the left are the instrument panel and a fire extinguisher. *Patton Museum*

This photo taken June 18, 1942, shows a few further details in the driver's station in an early-production M4A3, identified only as "PG [GM Proving Ground] #8037" (the Ford pilot M4A3 was GM PG #8029). To the left of the steering-brake levers is the clutch pedal; to the right of the driver's seat are the transmission gear-shift lever and the left side of the transmission. *Patton Museum*

The transmission and part of the assistant driver's station, including the mount for the bow machine gun and its equilibrator coil spring, are in view in the Ford pilot M4A3. Below the bow machine-gun mount is a holder for its ammunition box. To the left of the bow machine-gun mount is a horizontal groove in the glacis armor that corresponds to the horizontal ridge that existed on the exterior of the glacis of this pilot vehicle. This groove and the two cast-in brackets with holes in them, which straddle the groove, were part of the original design for a twin machine-gun mount to the left of the bow gun. *Patton Museum*

The assistant driver's station is viewed from behind the seat, in GM Proving Ground M4A3 #8037 on June 18, 1942, showing the brackets and groove for two machine guns from a different perspective. These guns appeared in very limited numbers early on in Sherman development. In the sponson to the right is a box for spare periscope heads. *Patton Museum*

At the heart of the M4A3 was the Ford GAA V-8, four-cycle, liquid-cooled engine. The GAA used gasoline, had a displacement of 1,100 cubic inches, and developed a maximum net horsepower of 450 at 2,600 rpm and 500 maximum gross horsepower at 2,600 rpm. A Ford GAA is viewed from the rear end, as it was installed in the tank. On the top are the two Bendix Stromberg NA-45G carburetors and their manifold, to the sides of which are the camshaft housings. In the foreground are the two four-cylinder magnetos. On the side is the left exhaust manifold. *Patton Museum*

The output end of a Ford GAA engine during endurance testing at Aberdeen Proving Ground on July 6, 1944. At the front is the bell housing, on each side of which is an engine mount. Above the bell housing is the exhaust tube, which is connected to both exhaust manifolds. The front carburetor is on top of the block, between the camshaft housings. *Patton Museum*

Ford Tank Arsenal workers at the Highland Park plant are guiding a turret with the 75 mm Gun M3 installed onto a Medium Tank M4A3 hull. Attached to the bottom of the turret is the turret basket, painted white inside and out, as was the interior of the turret. This model of turret was the D50878 type. *Benson Ford Archives*

Using a sling and an overhead crane, Ford mechanics on the final-assembly line are installing a GAA V-8 engine in the engine compartment of a Medium Tank M4A3. The man in the white sweater (*second from left*) has his left hand on the crankcase breather, above and between the magnetos. The number "23" is painted on the sponson and the rear of the upper hull. The man to the far left is standing on a plank attached to a rack that is hung on the rear plate of the upper hull. The tracks are the steel T49 type, with two short, horizontal grousers and one long one on each link. *Benson Ford Archives*

An M4A3 numbered "20" on the glacis is in the final part of assembly at Ford's Highland Park facility. By now, the rotor shield for the 75 mm gun was being produced with armored "cheeks" cast in, to better protect the barrel where it entered the shield. On the far side of the glacis is a bracket for mounting an extra antenna; note its tapered shape, narrower at the top. Ford installed the siren on the left bumper throughout the company's production of the small-hatch, dry-stowage M4A3. *Benson Ford Archives*

Workers are giving final touches to small-hatch, direct-vision M4A3s at Ford's Highland Park plant. The nearest tank is numbered "28." Early-style vane sights are visible on the turret roofs to the fronts of the hatches. The lead tank, and presumably the rest of them, have the single-piece final-drive assemblies, as the castings that contained the differential, the steering brakes, and the final-drive units were referred to. The tracks are the T41 model, with solid-rubber blocks with smooth surfaces. *Benson Ford Archives*

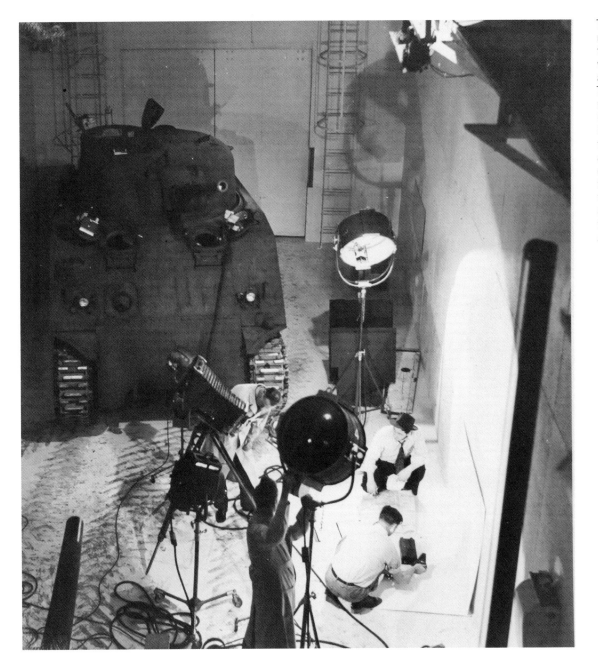

The story behind this photo is unknown, but the scenario is as follows. In the left background of a white-painted, closed chamber is a mint-condition Ford Medium Tank M4A3; to the lower left is the rear of a 3-inch Gun Motor Carriage M10A1, also produced by Ford; and one of the two men on the right is arranging a track block and an end connector so that they can be photographed. A large-format bellows camera is on a tripod to the front of the M4A3, and high-intensity floodlights are focused on the tableau. *Benson Ford Archives*

A Medium Tank M4A3, registration number 3055617 and Ordnance number 2657, is viewed from the right side during testing by the Armored Force Board at Fort Knox, Kentucky, in early August 1942. This was the third production M4A3, completed in August 1942. A Browning M2 HB .50-caliber machine gun is on a pintle mount on the hatch ring on the turret. The sprockets are the "dimpled" style, part number D47366A; the bogie wheels are the stamped, solid-spoked C85163 type; and the idler wheels are the open-spoke D37916 model. *Joe DeMarco collection*

The T49 tracks are fitted on a Medium Tank M4A3, registration number 3055617, during testing at Fort Knox in early August 1942. Cast into the upper center of the final-drive assembly is the part number of the armored housing, E4186. The drivers' hatch doors are open, and M6 periscopes are installed on the rotating mounts on them. *Joe DeMarco collection*

The design of the rear armored plate of the upper hull of Medium Tank M4A3, registration number 3055617, is displayed. An idler-adjusting wrench is stored on it. Below this plate is the exhaust deflector, with vanes built into it. On the rears of the sponsons are the two taillight assemblies with their brush guards. *Joe DeMarco collection*

Medium Tank M4A3, registration number 3055617, is observed from the upper left during tests by the Armored Force Board at Fort Knox in August 1942. The T-shaped grille/doors of the engine deck of the pilot M4A3 were replaced on the production vehicles by two grille/doors forming a rectangle. Each door had two grab handles on the inboard side of the frame. To the front of these grilles is a folded tarpaulin, stored atop an armored splash guard that encloses the armored filler covers for the two inner, vertical fuel tanks and the coolant surge tank. On the left side of that splash guard, and protected by a curved splash guard, is the cover for the left, horizontal fuel tank. Dimly visible below the pistol port of the turret is the cover for the filler for the auxiliary-generator fuel tank. *Joe DeMarco collection*

Three small-hatch, dry-stowage M4A3s from the 10th Tank Battalion, 5th Armored Division, are engaged in a training exercise at Fort Knox, Kentucky, in the fall of 1943. All three tanks have the early vane sights on the turrets and the narrow rotor shield with armored cheeks. *National Archives*

Ford Tank Arsenal workers are fabricating a small-hatch, dry-stowage M4A3 upper hull, which is secured to a jig. The man on top is running a grinder over the right side of the hull. At the lower right, a welder is operating on the area to the rear of the driver's hatch. Note the layout of the weld beads that join the sections of the glacis and the drivers' hoods. Rectangular cutouts in the hoods are for fixed M6 periscopes, while the round holes in the hatch doors are for rotating mounts for M6 periscopes. Equilibrator springs are attached to the hatch doors to make them easier to operate. The lifting eyes without pads on their bases were introduced after January 1943. *Benson Ford Archives*

After a drive over a test course that obviously included a mud hole, an unidentified driver of an M4A3 proudly shows off his mud-spattered overalls, tanker's helmet, and face. The final-drive assembly is the early version, with a rounded front and two single tow eyes. *Benson Ford Archives*

The crewmen of an M4A3 from the 10th Tank Battalion, 5th Armored Division, are on the alert during autumn 1943 maneuvers at Fort Knox. The tow cable and glare are obscuring the company letter on the left side of the final-drive assembly, but the white "16," representing the vehicle's number in the order of march, is in view. The T49 tracks, with their two short and two long grousers on each steel block, were better performers on soft ground and snow than were the T51 tracks, with smooth rubber blocks, that often were installed on Sherman tanks. *National Archives*

The assistant driver of this M4A3, assigned to the 10th Tank Battalion, has painted his name, "PFC. GEARY," in white with a stencil on the front of his hood. The photo was taken during training maneuvers in Kentucky in autumn 1943. A Browning M1919A4 .30-caliber machine gun is installed on a pintle mount on the turret hatch ring. *National Archives*

This small-hatch, dry-stowage Medium Tank M4A3 was part of the collection of the late Kevin Kronlund. It was fitted with appliqué armor plates on the fronts of the drivers' hoods and on the sponsons. The hoods were the type with direct-vision ports eliminated, since these were a weak point of the frontal armor. In the absence of direct-vision ports, fixed M6 periscopes were installed in the top fronts of the hoods; these were in addition to M6 periscopes on rotating mounts on the small-hatch doors.

The final-drive assembly has two double towing eyes, with solid, cast-in steps on their outboard sides. A siren with brush guard is on the left side of the glacis; a headlight assembly, with a blackout lamp on top of the service headlight, is mounted inside a brush guard on each side of the glacis. Nearly surrounding the bow machine-gun mount is a welded-on fitting for snapping on a dustcover over the machine gun.

The tracks are the T48 type, with rubber blocks with a chevron grouser on the outer face. The lifting eyes on the glacis have flared bottoms that are welded to the armor. The 75 mm gun barrel is resting on the travel lock, a feature that was introduced to Ford small-hatch M4A3s in July 1943.

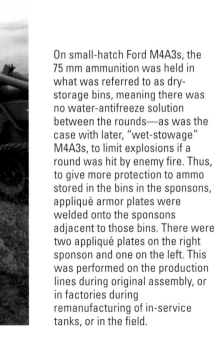

On small-hatch Ford M4A3s, the 75 mm ammunition was held in what was referred to as dry-storage bins, meaning there was no water-antifreeze solution between the rounds—as was the case with later, "wet-stowage" M4A3s, to limit explosions if a round was hit by enemy fire. Thus, to give more protection to ammo stored in the bins in the sponsons, appliqué armor plates were welded onto the sponsons adjacent to those bins. There were two appliqué plates on the right sponson and one on the left. This was performed on the production lines during original assembly, or in factories during remanufacturing of in-service tanks, or in the field.

As part of a rebuilding checklist during the Korean War, the center of the splash guard to the immediate front of the grille/doors on the engine deck was cut away, and torsion bars were installed on the sides of the grille/doors. The latter measure made it much easier to open the doors, which were very heavy. On the turret bustle are brackets for storing the .50-caliber machine gun during travel. Tack-welded to the bottom edge of the sponson is a strip for attaching a sand shield.

In a rear view of the tank, the rear brackets for the grille/door torsion bars are visible on the outboard rear corners of the engine deck. The cutout in the splash guard to the rear of the turret also is in view. A sledgehammer is stowed in its brackets near the rear of the engine deck.

When appliqué armor was welded on dry-stowage M4A3s, the left sponson normally received one armor plate, in the location shown here. The rail welded to the left side of the turret above the pistol port appears to have been a postwar modification.

The sprocket on this M4A3 is the version of the D47366 sprocket referred to as the "economy" model, since it lacked the intricate cutouts the other types of Sherman sprockets had. On the left side of the chassis, each of the three D47527 bogie brackets exhibits different mold lines and casting marks.

The front left bogie assembly is depicted, with solid-spoke bogie wheels installed. The bogie brackets, or bogie frames, support the suspension arms, the vertical volute springs, and the track-support roller arms. These frames were interchangeable as to the side of the vehicle they were mounted on, simply by screwing the arms for the track-support rollers on the other face of the brackets.

The same bogie assembly is viewed more to the rear. On top of the bogie frame is a steel skid. The track-support rollers on this tank are mounted above spacers, which are form-fitted to the support arms and act to raise the rollers slightly, to prevent wear to the tops of the skids.

The idler wheel is the solid-spoke, stamped-steel C85164 type. On opposite sides of the wheel surface are a slightly recessed grease plug and a relief valve. An excellent view is presented of the end connectors of the track. Each of these connectors was secured to two adjacent track pins by a wedge bolt and a locknut.

The appliqué armor was attached to the sponsons with built-up weld beads around the sides and top, forming a beveled surface. Also in view are the weld beads between the glacis and the side of the sponson.

Details of the left taillight and its brush guard, the left rear lifting eye, and the weld seams of the armor plates are in view. The oblong panel with the hex bolt on its center, between the lifting eye and the brush guard, is the cover for the left grouser compartment, a space in the hull for storing grousers: metal appliances that were attached to the tracks to improve traction on snow, ice, and soft ground.

The exhaust deflector on the rear of the hull was fabricated from sheet metal and was hinged so as to swing up, for accessing the engine-compartment door and other features on the rear of the lower hull. The engine-compartment door on the M4A3 was a single-piece unit, with two hinges on the left side.

Details of the forward-right appliqué armor plate on the M4A3 are displayed. On the roof above the appliqué armor is the armored splash guard of the assistant driver's ventilator.

The assistant driver's cast hood, with a hinged lid for a fixed M6 periscope to the front of the small-hatch door, is viewed from above, also showing the weld beads on the top of the appliqué armor plate on the front of the hood. On the hatch door is a round, rotating base for another M6 periscope, with the lid for the periscope open. The brush guard on this rotating mount, fabricated from welded steel rods, were introduced to the M4A3 production line at the Ford plant in August 1943.

The travel lock for the 75 mm gun barrel became a part of the Ford assembly-line process for the M4A3 during July 1943. On the glacis behind the travel lock is a sprung hold-down latch for the travel lock. To the right is the driver's cast hood, fixed periscope lid, and small-hatch door. Below the grab handle on the door is a padlock hasp. The double-hook-shaped bracket on the inboard side of the driver's armored hood was for securing the driver's foul-weather hood, a canvas cover with a glass windshield.

Engine Data	
Engine make/model	Ford GAA
Number of cylinders	V-8
Cubic-inch displacement	1,100
Horsepower	500 @ 2,600 rpm
Gross torque	1040 @ 2,200 rpm

In an overall view of the driver's cast-armor hood and small hatch, another double-hook bracket for the foul-weather hood is on the outboard side of the armored hood. Note the hold-open latch on the hatch door, on the outboard side of the rotating periscope. To the side of the driver's hatch is his ventilator hood and surrounding splash guard. To the rear of the ventilator is a tow-cable holder.

Viewed from the turret roof of the Kronlund M4A3 are, *from the bottom*, the 75 mm gun shield and rotor shield with cheeks; the drivers' ventilators, hoods, and hatches, with rotating and fixed periscopes; the travel lock; the forward antenna bracket (*right*); the front lifting eyes; and the headlights, siren, and brush guards. The equilibrator springs, to assist the drivers in opening the hatch doors, were not present on the earliest small hatches.

The rotor shield (or mantlet), part number D51288, with built-in cheeks to the sides, and the gun shield, part number D50880, which was screwed to the front of the turret, were part of the Combination Gun Mount M34, upon which the 75 mm Gun M3 was installed. The coaxial .30-caliber M1919A4 machine gun, protruding through a slot in the gun shield, has the early-type outer jacket with cooling slots, instead of the small, round holes used on the later jackets. Two lifting eyes are welded to the top of the gun shield.

The turret roof is viewed from the front, with the gunner's periscope hood and a late-type vane sight to the front of the hatch. To the right is the turret ventilator hood and splash guard. The .50-caliber machine gun barrel is secured to a travel lock on the front of the hatch ring. On each of the split doors of the hatch are hold-open latches. On one door is a rotating mount for an M6 periscope, including a periscope lid and brush guard. A grab handle is on the other door. In the background, an antenna is mounted on the recessed, left antenna bracket.

From another angle over the front of the turret of the small-hatch, dry-stowage M4A3(75), the square-shaped, slightly recessed right radio antenna bracket is visible on the rear of the turret roof, below the ammunition-box holder for the .50-caliber machine gun. The grooves next to the hinges on the hatch ring are to provide clearance for installing or removing the hinge pins.

In a final view from above the front of the turret, in the foreground is the front lifting ring, with the ventilator and its splash guard to the rear of it. The loader's rotating periscope mount is on the left side of the roof. A late-style vane sight is in the left foreground.

As photographed from atop the engine deck of the M4A3, in the foreground are the air-intake grille/doors, to the front of which are armored splash guards to protect the fuel-filler and surge-tank-filler caps as well as the base of the turret. The grille/doors are formed from steel rods welded to the frame, with cross-reinforcing provided by weld beads. Both radio antenna brackets on the rear of the roof of the turret are in sight.

The engine deck is seen from above the rear of the turret roof, with the travel bracket for the .50-caliber machine gun at the center. The torsion bars on the sides of the grille/doors are a Korean War modification, to make it easier to lift and close the heavy doors. A sledgehammer and an idler wrench are stored in brackets on the rear plate of the engine deck. Note the three lateral reinforcements on each grille, formed from weld beads.

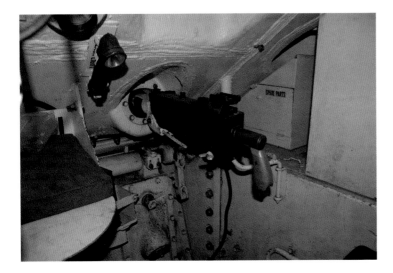

In the assistant driver's station, to the left is a shelf for storing the driver's foul-weather hood, and to the right is the bow machine gun, a Browning M1919A4 .30-caliber type. A flashlight is on a clip bracket next to the machine gun. In the front of the sponson to the right is a spare-parts box, above which is the interior of the forward antenna bracket on the glacis.

As seen from above the transmission facing to the rear, to the left is the assistant driver's seat, to the bottom right is the driveshaft tunnel, and to the upper right is the lower part of the turret basket, below which is a dry-stowage bin for 75 mm ammunition.

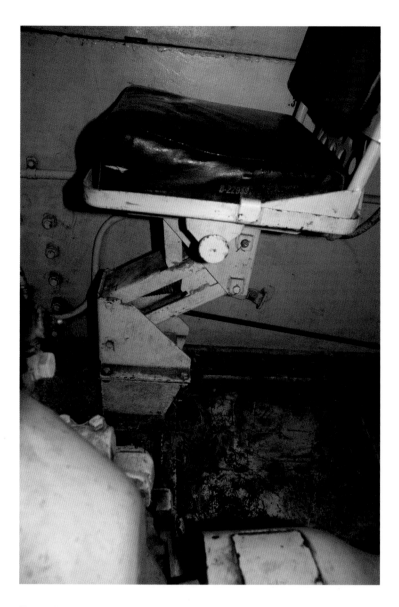

The assistant driver's seat is viewed from its left side, showing the adjustable support that enabled the occupant to sit with head down in the hull or above the hatch. On the floor to the rear of this seat was an escape hatch, which, on this vehicle, has been replaced by a plain piece of metal. The original hatch had two grab handles, four locking rods, and an operating lever.

The gunner's seat, mounted on the right side of the turret basket, is adjustable for height and front-to-rear. The red T-shaped handle above the seat is the turret lock.

The elevation and traversing controls and the azimuth indicator are seen from a closer perspective. Below the elevation handwheel is the hydraulic traversing mechanism, with its control box on the right side, the motor at the center, and the hydraulic reservoir on the left. The black object to the rear of the control box is the handgrip for the hydraulic traversing control.

In a photo taken above the gunner's seat, at the top is the gunner's periscope, with a mechanical link down to the gun mount to enable the periscope to tilt in unison with the elevation of the gun. Below the periscope are the gun elevation handwheel (*left*), the manual traversing handle (*center*), and the azimuth indicator (*right*), which provides the azimuth of the 75 mm gun with reference to the longitudinal centerline of the tank.

The commander's round, folding seat is mounted on the turret, near which are intercom control boxes and wiring, a microphone, and headphones. In the turret bustle to the right is the radio set, above which is a bin for .45-caliber ammunition for a Thompson submachine gun.

The rear bulkhead and, *right*, the rear of the left sponson are viewed through an opening in the turret basket. To the left is part of the oil cooler; the fixture to the side of it with four holes on it is for the fuel shutoff valve knobs, which are not installed. At the center is the left air cleaner, with the air duct to the carburetor being routed from the top of the air cleaner through the top of the bulkhead. The dark-colored object in the sponson is the auxiliary generator.

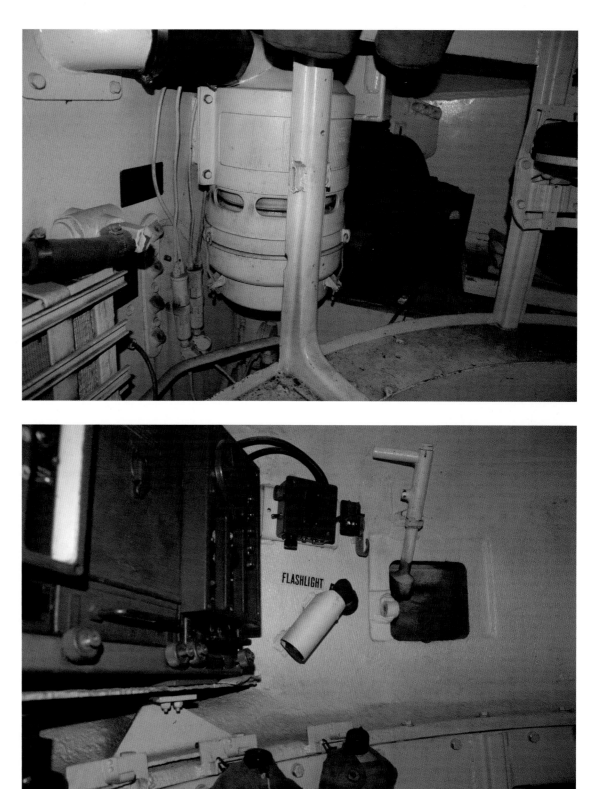

The radio set is to the left, with an intercom control box, flashlight holder, and pistol port adjacent to it. The L-shaped operating handle is attached to the pistol-port cover; when the cover was opened, a lug on the handle was inserted into the eye welded to the left side of the port, to keep the cover open. Canteens are stored at the bottom of the photo.

FLASHLIGHT

Reenactors are manning a small-hatch, dry-stowage M4A3, registration number 3054537, in the collection of Brent Mullins. Period-accurate T48 tracks, with rubber blocks with chevron grousers, are installed. The final-drive assembly is the early, single-piece type, with two single tow eyes.

Although the Mullins M4A3 has the torsion bars for the engine-air grille/doors, a Korean War modification, it lacks the associated cutout in the center of the splash guard to the immediate front of those grilles.

The high-bustle turret on the Mullins small-hatch, dry-stowage M4A3 is an anomaly, since it was developed for large-hatch hulls.

Details such as the two right appliqué plates, the strip on the bottom of the sponson for screwing on the sand shield, and elements of the bow, glacis, and suspension are viewed from the front right.

The bogie wheels on the Mullins M4A3 are the D38501 open-spoke pattern with steel plugs spot-welded over the openings. This was done per Technical Bulletin TB ORD 22, of January 28, 1944, and was in response to reports of enemy troops thrusting steel bars or rods into the openings of the wheels in order to immobilize the tanks.

The Mullins small-hatch, dry-stowage M4A3 is parked in the foreground alongside an M4A1 and an M4A3(76)W with horizontal-volute suspension system (HVSS). Above the front lifting eye on the roof of the M4A3 is a spotlight, turned downward.

Weld seams that join the armor plates of the sponson and the rear of the upper hull are visible. The exhaust deflector under the rear of the upper hull is the early type, fabricated from sheet metal. Later in production, an armored exhaust deflector would be used.

The M4A3 is seen from the front while in motion. The board across the final-drive assembly replicates those often installed on Sherman tanks to form an equipment rack, or as a retainer to hold sandbag armor in place on the glacis.

The two appliqué armor plates on the right side of the sponson of a small-hatch, dry-stowage Medium Tank M4A3 in the collection of Brent Mullins are depicted, showing the weld beads that form beveled edges around the sides and tops of the plates. On the assistant driver's hatch door, note the hold-open latch, secured to a notched lug welded to the hull.

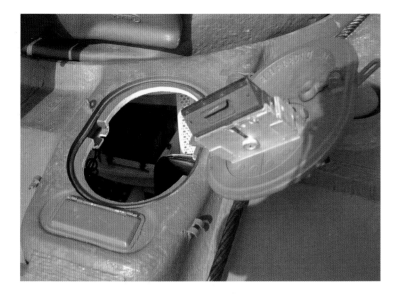

The driver's hatch door is open, showing the rotating mount for the M6 periscope on it. The ring toggle on the outboard side of the interior of the door is for latching the door; to accomplish this, it engages the cutout in the recessed bracket on the opposite side of the hatch. A weather seal is around the inner ledge of the hatch, and on the sides of the driver's hood are two small brackets for attaching the foul-weather hood. To the front of the hatch is the lid, with a piano hinge, for the fixed M6 periscope.

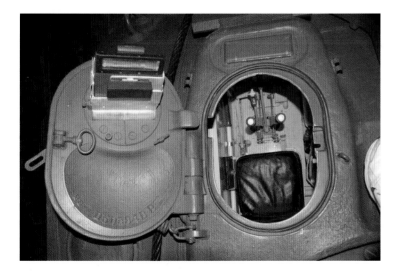

An M6 periscope is inserted in the holder on the rotating mount on the driver's hatch door. Note the dull-black crash pad on the periscope. Visible inside the hatch are the driver's seat, the steering-brake levers, and, to the left of the seat, a spare periscope in a holder. Note the small clevis that secures the equilibrator spring of the hatch door to an eye welded to the driver's hood.

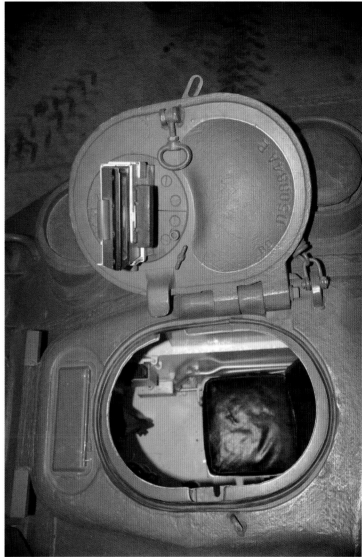

The hatch door for the assistant driver is open, showing his seat inside the hull. Cast onto the bulge on the door, which was intended to give the occupant slightly more headroom, is its part number, D50884A. The ring-shaped toggle latch on the door, and its mating notch on the rim of the hatch, are apparent. A T-shaped release handle for the turret hold-open latch is on the opposite side of the periscope from the door-locking ring.

The thickened armor of the front right quarter of the turret has a ledge at the bottom, where the armor becomes thinner. That ledge is visible here in the form of a shadow toward the bottom of the turret. The vane sight on the right front of the turret roof is the late type, with a J-shaped sight, perforated with peep holes, attached to a bracket that is welded to the roof.

The D68454 rotor shield (mantlet) is fastened in place with slotted, oval-headed screws that are countersunk into the armor. Casting marks are adjacent to the port for the coaxial machine gun; on the opposite side is the port for the gunner's telescopic sight. The armored cheeks on the shield to the sides of the 75 mm gun barrel have a slight curve when viewed from the front.

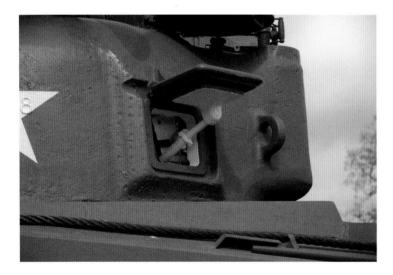

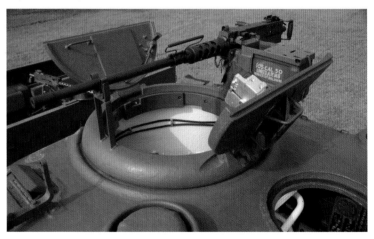

The cover for the pistol port on the high-bustle turret is open, held in place by the operating handle that is visible inside the port. The groove in the armor above the port is for inserting or removing the hinge pin for the cover of the port. The lifting ring to the rear of the pistol port has a nearly flat inner perimeter.

The right hatch of the high-bustle turret is displayed, with the loader's port to the lower right, through which the recoil guard of the 75 mm gun and the radio set are visible. This type of hatch assembly, called the race assembly in the Ordnance Supply Catalog for the M4 series, was assigned part number D51050. The barrel of the .50-caliber machine gun is resting in the spring clamp on top of the travel lock, welded to the hatch ring. Note the handle on the gun barrel, which was helpful when removing a red-hot barrel from the gun's receiver. On the closer door of the right hatch, the silver-colored object is the holder for the commander's rotating M6 periscope.

The two hatches on the turret are viewed from the front. The Olive Drab M6 periscope is in the silver-colored holder on the right hatch. On the door for the loader's hatch is a locking bolt. The loader's hatch was assigned part number C101570.

On the rear of the high-bustle turret roof are, *left*, a round, recessed bracket with a rim around it, for mounting a radio antenna, and, *right*, a raised, block-shaped antenna bracket with a cover screwed to its top. Footman loops were welded to the bustle, for strapping gear in place. Below the lower left corner of the bustle is the housing for the two pull handles for the fixed fire-extinguisher system. The splash guard below the bustle has a jog in it to provide room for these handles and their housing. Below the lifting eye on the left side of the bustle is the armored cover for the fuel filler for the auxiliary generator.

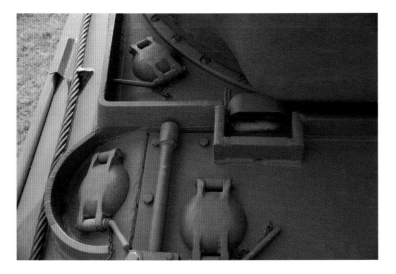

The left-hand armored filler caps are shown close-up, with the two caps for the fillers for the two left fuel tanks at the bottom, separated by the front end of a torsion bar, and the cap for the auxiliary-generator fuel filler at the top. These caps were hinged on one side and secured with a bent pin on the other. To the right are the pull handles for the fire extinguisher.

With the split doors of the turret hatch open, the recoil guard of the 75 mm Gun M3 is visible inside, along with the gunner's seat cushion and some of the gun's controls. The hatch was installed on a race, so that it could be rotated freely. On the left side of the hatch ring is the hatch lock.

This is a gunner's view of the interior of the M4A3(75) turret, with the 75 mm gun's recoil guard to the left, the elevation handwheel and manual-traversing hand crank and their associated gears to the center, and the azimuth indicator at the right. Above the elevating and traversing controls are the direct sight and its L-shaped crash pad, *left*, and the gunner's periscope, *right*.

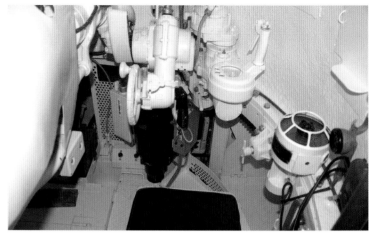

More details of the gunner's station are displayed. Below the elevation handwheel is the hydraulic traversing mechanism, the centerpiece of which is the cylinder-shaped motor, with the hydraulic oil pump below it. On the left side of the motor is the hydraulic-oil reservoir; mounted on the right side of the motor is a box with switches for the turret, the stabilizer, and firing. The black grip to the right of the elevation handwheel is the control handle for powered traverse. To the right, to the front of the azimuth indicator is the turret lock. On the floor to the left of the hydraulic motor are the firing switches for the 75 mm and coaxial guns, to the left of which is the manual firing pedal for the 75 mm gun.

An SCR-528 radio installation in the turret bustle of the Mullins M4A3 is pictured. To the left is the BC-604 radio transmitter, at the center is the CH-264 chest, and to the right is the BC-603 receiver set. At the top is a rack for .45-caliber ammunition clips for a Thompson submachine gun.

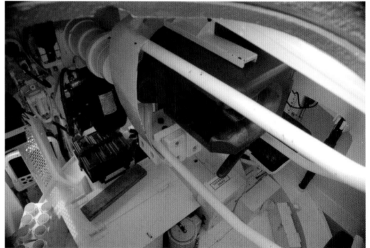

In a wide-angle view of the turret through the loader's hatch, in the foreground are the 75 mm gun, its recoil guard, and its recoil and carriage assembly. Above the three stored machine-gun ammunition boxes toward the left is a black mechanism: this is the gyrostabilizer control and gear box, which worked with the dark-colored cylinder to the upper left to maintain the 75 mm gun at a constant elevation with reference to true horizontal, even while the tank was in movement. To the front of the turret basket to the left is the driver's seat; storage racks for 2-inch smoke-mortar rounds are at the lower left.

The smoke-mortar-round racks seen in the lower left in the preceding photo are seen again, with a portable fire extinguisher secured next to them. At the upper center is the ammunition box and holder for the .30-caliber coaxial machine gun.

The engine compartment of the Mullins M4A3 is viewed from the rear, with the fan shrouds at the bottom. The air-intake manifold has been removed from the carburetors; the front ends of the manifold, when installed, are connected to the two round ducts on the front bulkhead, which are connected to the air cleaners in the rear of the fighting compartment. In the front corners of the engine compartment are the two vertical fuel tanks.

The engine compartment is observed from the left side, with the fan shrouds to the right, and the right vertical fuel tank in the background. Two carburetors are supplied, one mounted on the front and the other on the rear of the top of the engine. In the foreground is the left camshaft housing, with a removable rectangular plate on top for accessing the spark plugs.

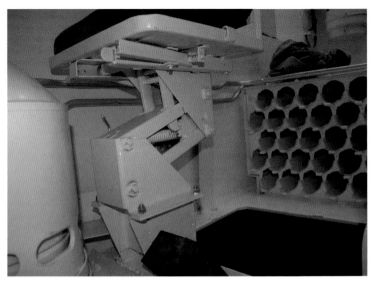

The driver's seat and controls are viewed from the lower front, with the accelerator pedal in the left foreground and the steering-brake levers to the front of the driver's seat. The turret has been removed from the hull, allowing a clear view into the rear of the fighting compartment, with the right air cleaner and an ammunition bin to the left and the oil cooler on the bulkhead adjacent to the air cleaner.

Details of the assistant driver's seat pedestal are in view. The pedestal included mechanisms for lifting the seat and sliding it back and forth. To the rear of the seat, the escape hatch has been removed, and behind the open hatch is a dry-storage 75 mm ammunition bin. (The object to the left is an air cleaner, temporarily placed there.)

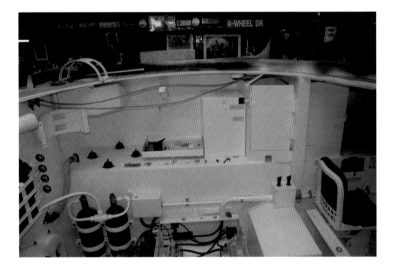

With the turret of the Mullins M4A3 removed, the left side of the fighting compartment is in full view. To the left on the rear bulkhead are the oil cooler, four red-colored fuel-shutoff handles, the curved bracket for the left air cleaner, and the auxiliary-generator fuel tank. In the sponson are four cushioned mountings for the auxiliary generator (not installed) and several lockers, including one marked for a cook stove and rations. On the hull floor at the center of the photo is the battery box, to the rear of which are the two fixed fire extinguishers. To the right is the driver's seat.

The interior of the turret basket of the Mullins M4A3 is viewed through an opening in its left front, with the gunner's seat and pedestal to the left, the folded seat for the commander to the rear of the gunner's seat, and stored ammunition boxes in the foreground. To the right is a perforated panel of the basket. Visible through openings in the rear of the basket is the rear bulkhead of the fighting compartment, including the right air cleaner and the oil cooler.

As seen from above the driver's seat, the turret basket is to the right, the escape hatch and part of the transmission are to the bottom, and the assistant driver's seat is in the left background. Stored 75 mm ammunition is in the rack below the turret basket.

The driver's foul-weather hood is stored on a rack above the transmission. The hood was secured over the driver's hatch to give him a weatherproof enclosure, with a glass windshield, during inclement weather. To the left of this hood is the primer, below which is the hand throttle.

General Data

Model	M4A3	M4A3(76)W	M4A3(105) HVSS
Weight*	66,700	74,200	72,900
Length**	232.5	297	247
Width**	103	118	118
Height**	108	117	115.7
Tread	83	89	89
Crew	5	5	5
Maximum speed (mph)	26	26	26
Fuel capacity (gallons)	168	168	168
Range (miles)	130	100	100
Electrical (volts)	24	24	24
Transmission speeds	5F	1R	
	5F	1R	
	5F	1R	
Turning			
Radius (feet)	31	31	31
Armament	main	secondary	flexible

* Fighting weight
** Overall dimensions listed in inches

Communication Equipment

M4 Sherman vehicles were provided with SCR-508, SCR-528, or SCR-538 in the rear of the turret. Command tanks also had a sponson-mounted SCR-506. All basic radios were provided with integral interphone. Flag set M238 and panel set AP50A were also provided.

CHAPTER 2
M4A3 Large-Hatch, Wet-Stowage Tanks

In 1943, it was decided that the Sherman's design would be significantly improved and its construction streamlined. Other than the M4A4, all subsequent versions of the Sherman would be built as large-hatch vehicles. Ten different plants turned out the small-hatch Shermans, but only three factories made the large-hatch versions: Chrysler Defense Arsenal, Fisher Tank Arsenal, and Pressed Steel Car Company. All three of these makers were producing Shermans when the larger hatch was introduced to production in increments, as will be seen later.

On the large-plate Shermans, one larger plate, pitched at a 47-degree angle, replaced the earlier design feature of multiple front plates. Hatch bulges disappeared on the large-plate version, and the hatches were enlarged to facilitate entering and exiting the tank. Inserted in between the hatches was a large ventilator designed to allow the exit of gases produced by weapons fire.

Apart from vehicles armed with 105 mm weapons, most of the new tanks featured "wet" ammunition storage, internally. Specially designed ammunition containers that incorporated fluid jackets were used to store the shells for the main gun. Intended to prevent ammunition fires, these containers have become a distinguishing feature for the large-hull tanks, which are sometimes called "wet-storage tanks." The small-hatch tanks lacked such wet-storage ammunition containers and therefore are often dubbed "dry-storage tanks." In actuality, though, dry ammunition storage did feature on a few of the very early large-hatch Shermans.

In February 1944, under production order T-9724, Fisher Tank Arsenal commenced manufacture of the M4A3 with registration number 3081212. All the 75 mm M4A3 tanks were produced by Fisher Tank Arsenal, which was already turning out the large-hatch M4A2. Since both vehicles were present on the production line at the same time, the two tank types shared some common traits in construction.

The complex engine deck design of the large-hatch tank was simplified by the elimination of two of the fuel filler caps. The bullet splash rail was scaled down to a triangular frame around the oil tank filler cap.

A unique feature of the Fisher Tank Arsenal M4A3 tanks produced at this period was the split engine deck. The earlier, dry-stowage M4A3 vehicles' rearmost deck section was revised and divided into two sections.

Production of the 76 mm armed M4A3 began at Chrysler's Detroit Tank Arsenal in March 1944. Features of the new vehicle were an updated hull, bigger hatches for the driver and codriver, and a simpler single-piece glacis armor plate. Apart from its ammunition racks, the hull and drivetrain were identical to those on the 75 mm armed version. To reduce risk of fire in case of penetration of the hull, the ammunition stowage was moved from the hull sponsons and enclosed in water tanks. These tanks were at first manufactured with the smooth-barrel M1A1 76 mm gun, but later variations on these vehicles were fitted with the M1A1C or M1A2 gun, with the possibility of a muzzle brake being added.

Later-production turrets also began to incorporate a provision for fitting a canvas cover to seal out dust from the openings around the rotor shield of the outer gun. Although the 76 mm gun was able to penetrate about one more inch of armor thickness than the 75 mm gun could pierce at a comparable range, its high-explosive round was not as effective as that of the 75 mm. Accordingly, the 75 mm M4A3 continued to be manufactured. Only when supplies of the tungsten-core HVAP ammunition became sufficient was the 76 mm gun able to counter the frontal armor of the German Panther at battlefield range.

Armored units began to receive M4A3 (76) W tanks in the fall of 1944. They were preceded in service by the M4A1 (76) because the logistics for supplying spare parts for the new Ford power plant, which had never seen service in Europe, had to be established. Nevertheless, by the later stages of the European war, the M4A3 was the most common tank in the American armored divisions and independent tank battalions.

A total of 4,542 of the M4A3 76 mm tanks were produced before production ended in April 1945. Both Chrysler Tank Arsenal and the General Motors Fisher Body assembly plant manufactured the vehicles. The first 1,400 of the tanks featured the narrow track and original style of volute spring suspension.

In February 1944, a revamped upper hull would go into production for the M4A3, which, in order to save time on the assembly line, would incorporate a single-plate glacis, set at 47 degrees from vertical, and large hatches for the driver and the assistant driver. These vehicles also deleted the 75 mm ammunition racks in the sponsons, replacing them with bins on the floor, which were filled with water-antifreeze solution, to limit the damage if an enemy projectile struck one of the ammunition rounds. This arrangement was referred to as wet stowage; hence, these tanks were designated M4A3(75)W, the "W" standing for wet stowage. Shown here is the pilot M4A3(75)W, registration number 3054578, which started out as a small-hatch, dry-stowage vehicle from Ford's July 1943 production. As seen in a February 8, 1944, photo, for this conversion a wedge of steel plate was welded to the front of each of the sponsons, to arrive at the 47 degrees required for the glacis. *FCA North America Archives*

The sole manufacturer of the large-hatch, wet-stowage Medium Tank M4A3(75)W with vertical-volute suspension system (VVSS) was the Fisher Tank Arsenal, which delivered 2,420 units. The example portrayed here, registration number 3081666 and Ordnance number 49069, is shown during testing by the Ordnance Operation, General Motors Proving Ground, on April 13, 1944. *Patton Museum*

As seen in a right-side photo of registration number 3081666, in addition to the steeper slope of the glacis, another recognition feature of the M4A3(75)W was the presence of hump-shaped hinges for the large-hatch doors to the front of the turret. The thickness of the armor of the glacis was increased from the 2 inches of the dry-stowage, small-hatch M4A3 to 2.5 inches. *Patton Museum*

The engine deck of the wet-stowage M4A3(75)W remained similar to that of the dry-stowage version, except for revisions to the splash guard between the grille/doors and the turret. The new, large hatches are somewhat visible in the shadow cast by the turret. The turret on this tank was the new D78461 model, with a redesigned bustle, the bottom of which was higher to clear the hinges of the drivers' hatches, and the top of which had less of a downward slope. The D78461 turret also had a new, oblong hatch on the roof for the loader. On the rear of the upper hull was a folding rack for storing bedrolls and gear. *Patton Museum*

Footman loops welded to the bustle were for strapping the commander's .50-caliber machine gun to the turret rear when it was not in use. Below the lower left corner of the bustle is the housing for the two pull handles for the fixed fire-extinguisher system. The splash guard below the bustle has a jog in it to provide room for these handles and their housing. Below the lifting eye on the side of the bustle is the armored cover for the fuel filler for the auxiliary generator. *Patton Museum*

In a rear view of a Medium Tank M4A3(75)W under evaluation by the Armored Force Board, at Fort Knox, Kentucky, the newly devised armored exhaust deflector is present below the rear of the upper hull. This replaced the earlier sheet-metal deflector, which was prone to being damaged. The armored deflector constituted two assemblies, mounted side by side on top hinges. Note also the racks on the rears of the sponsons for three spare track blocks apiece. *Patton Museum*

A restored Medium Tank M4A3(75)W nicknamed "BLOCKBUSTER," in the collection of the Patton Museum, is under motion during a reenactment. This tank bears the registration number 3082402 in Blue Drab on the sponson. The final-drive assembly is a later model, with a less rounded front than the early type, and is also equipped with dual tow eyes with welded-on steps. Note the rather rough machining on the bottom of the thickened part of the turret, below the recognition star. On the inboard side of the driver's head is a feature that was new for the M4A3(75)W: a ventilator between the drivers' hatches. The barrel of the .50-caliber machine gun is fitted with a decidedly non–World War II blank-firing device.

Early in the production of the M4A3(75)W, the top edge of the glacis was milled to a beveled shape so that it ran flush with the roof of the drivers' compartment. A close examination of the photo shows that the finish on the top of the glacis of this tank is the later type: square cut, with the front of the glacis protruding a bit above the roof of the hull.

Exhaust smoke is emanating from the exhaust deflector below the rear of the upper hull. The deflector is the sheet-metal type, not armored. The bogie wheels are a mix of the D52861 smooth-concave and the D78450 smooth-convex models, both of which were fabricated from stamped steel.

The driver's and assistant driver's hatch doors stood nearly vertically when open; in that position, and, if viewed from above, the profile of the doors tilted to the outside at their fronts.

The arms for the track-support rollers are the upswept type, designed to hold the tracks slightly above the steel skids attached to the tops of the bogie brackets, to reduce wear on the skids.

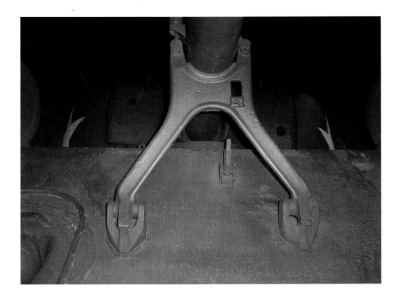

The travel lock of the M4A3(75)W currently nicknamed "BLOCKBUSTER" is viewed from the front. The rectangular opening on the travel lock was for engaging the hold-down latch, which is welded to the hull to the rear of the lock. *Don Moriarty*

Part of the turret and the driver's hatch of "BLOCKBUSTER" are depicted. Cast into the roof of the driver's compartment in the foreground, to the rear of the hatch door, is the trademark of the manufacturer, American Steel Foundries' Cast Armor Plant, East Chicago, Indiana: a letter *C* inside an octagon. Next to the trademark are casting numbers, including the part number, E8020. *Don Moriarty*

The assistant driver's hatch on "BLOCKBUSTER" is open, showing the rotating periscope mount and the casting numbers on the inner surface. The circular shape on the hull roof to the rear of the open hatch door was the location for a bracket for an additional radio antenna; this feature has been sealed with a plug. *Don Moriarty*

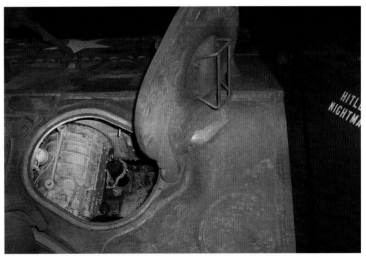

The transmission is visible below in a view of the open hatch of the assistant driver. A brush guard fabricated from welded steel rods is bolted to the rotating mount for the periscope on the hatch door. *Don Moriarty*

The M4A3 received an important upgrade when it was fitted with a new turret with a 76 mm Gun M1A1 in the Combination Mount M62. Although the 76 mm Gun M1A1 lacked the power of many of the other contemporaneous Allied and German antitank guns, it packed more of a punch than the Sherman's 75 mm Gun M3. The pilot for the M4A3(76)W, the wet-stowage, 76 mm armed version, was this small-hatch, composite-hull Ford M4A3(75), registration number 3054892, onto which a large-hatch, cast, forward hull was grafted. A new cupola with six glass vision blocks and a single, round hatch door has replaced the old hatch with split doors. The photo was taken on February 8, 1944.
FCA North America Archives

A Medium Tank M4A3(76)W, registration number 30100342 and Ordnance number 44018, displays the distinctive mantlet that was developed for the 76 mm gun's turret. For this weapon's Combination Mount M62, a rotor was not a part of the mechanism, so the mantlet was referred to officially as the gun shield. A lifting eye was incorporated into each side of the shield. This vehicle was completed by Chrysler Tank Arsenal in June 1944. This arsenal was the major producer of the M4A3(76)W, completing 4,017 examples with either VVSS or HVSS from March 1944 to April 1945. Fisher Tank Arsenal produced 525 M4A3(76)Ws with VVSS. *FCA North America Archives*

This vehicle, M4A3(76)W, registration number 30100252, also from Chrysler's June 1944 production, is armed with the 76 mm Gun M1A1C, which was distinguished by the protective sleeve screwed onto the threaded end of the barrel. The threads were for installing muzzle brakes, as they became available. The sides of the gun shield had rounded cutouts for accessing the trunnions of the gun carriage. The travel lock for the 76 mm gun was approximately 4 inches taller than the one for the 75 mm gun. *Patton Museum*

This Medium Tank M4A3(76)W, registration number 30100461 and ordnance number 44227, was the last of the June 1944 Chrysler vehicles of that model. It is shown on June 20, 1944, during testing by the Ordnance Operation, General Motors Proving Ground. The turret had a pistol port on the left side and an armored, arch-shaped ventilator hood on the center rear of the turret bustle. The rectangular object on the sponson to the front of the rear lifting eye is a stop for the left door/grille; a similar stop is on the opposite sponson. *Patton Museum*

CHAPTER 3
A New Suspension System Is Introduced

The horizontal-volute suspension system and its 23-inch-wide track were introduced in late 1944 and worked their way into production of the M4A3 in 1945. Sometimes called the E8 suspension, this system featured horizontal, instead of vertical, volute springs. For this reason, it was called the HVSS rather than the earlier VVSS (which stood for vertical-volute suspension system). The new tank, with its HVSS system, dual wheels, and significantly wider track, offered better cross-country performance, since ground pressure had been cut from 14 psi to approximately 11 psi.

The new suspension system was released for production in April 1944, and by September all Chrysler-built tanks were equipped with HVSS when they left the assembly line. Pressed Steel Car Company and Fisher Body Company completed adoption of HVSS by January 1, 1945. It is believed that Fisher Body built about 650 M4A3 (75) Shermans with the HVSS. Production of the M4A3 (76) with HVSS would continue until April 1945, at which time 2,617 had been completed.

Chrysler developed a new suspension system in mid-1943, referred to as the E8 and designated the horizontal-volute suspension system: a reference to the horizontal orientation of the two volute spring assemblies incorporated into each bogie assembly. A pilot tank with this suspension system was ready by December 1943, and the system was authorized for installation on M4A3(76)Ws by April 1944. Chrysler was the sole producer of this model of tank with HVSS. As seen on this example, each bogie unit included two dual wheels. The tracks on this vehicle are the single-pin T66 type, 23 inches in width. *Patton Museum*

The wider suspension of the M4A3(76)W with HVSS required the installation of fenders, which were supported by braces that were bolted to bosses welded to the sponsons. Wider sprockets and idler-wheel assemblies also were used. The registration number near the rear of the sponson appears to be 3031695, which represents a vehicle from Chrysler's September 1944 production. Between the pairs of dual bogie wheels are the bottoms of the bogie brackets, above which are the outer horizontal-volute-spring assemblies. *Patton Museum*

An M4A3(76)W with HVSS under testing by the Armored Force Board at Fort Knox, Kentucky, has a rolled tarpaulin strapped to the bedroll rack and a roll of camouflage net secured to the engine deck. The design of the rear mud flaps is apparent. Note the .50-caliber machine gun, broken down for storage on the turret bustle. The pintle cradle attached to the machine gun receiver is inserted in a bracket on the left side of the ventilator hood. The barrel of the gun is stored on clips on angle irons welded to the rear of the turret bustle. *Patton Museum*

The same M4A3(76)W depicted in the preceding photo is viewed from the right rear at Fort Knox. The nickname "TOM THUMB" and the number "458" are painted on the sponson. Three spare track links are stored on the sponson. *Patton Museum*

As seen in a right-side view of the same tank, "M4E8" is stenciled twice, once upside down, on the sand shield. Above each horizontal volute spring is a shock absorber, or snubber, which is connected to the tops of the suspension arms. The track-return rollers are mounted on spindles attached to the lower hull; there are three single rollers, above the shock absorbers, and two dual rollers. *Patton Museum*

Medium Tank M4A3(76)W with HVSS registration number 30123413 was part of Chrysler Tank Arsenal's March 1945 production. The main weapon is a 76 mm Gun M1A2, which had two principal distinguishing characteristics: it was fitted with a muzzle brake (seen here with a dustcover on it), and its rifling was slightly different than that used on the 76 mm Gun M1A1 and M1A1C. A dustcover also is installed over the gun shield. *Patton Museum*

This Medium Tank M4A3(76)W with HVSS, registration number 30113667 and Ordnance number 60645, was part of Chrysler Tank Arsenal's November 1944 production. Rearview mirrors, attached to the glacis just above both of the lifting eyes, were commonly found on M4A3(76)Ws. Note the machining on the lower several inches of the turret; there were variations in this feature from turret manufacturer to manufacturer. *Patton Museum*

On March 30, 1945, Medium Tank M4A3(76)W with HVSS registration number 30123402 exhibits mud on its bogies during a pause in testing at the Chrysler Tank Arsenal Proving Ground, Warren, Michigan. A close study of the photo reveals that the top edge of the glacis has the square-cut finish. *Patton Museum*

The same vehicle, registration number 30123402, is seen from the left rear during tests on March 30, 1945. The tracks on this vehicle were the double-pin T80 model, with steel shoes incorporating chevron grousers, and bonded-rubber inner pads. Although the T80 tracks saw very limited use in the final days of World War II, the T66 tracks being by far the most commonly used on HVSS tanks during the war, the T80s and the T84 rubber-block tracks would supplant the T66 tracks in the postwar years. *Patton Museum*

A Medium Tank M4A3(76)W with HVSS nicknamed "GIDEON," in the collection of Fred Kager, pauses during a reenactment. This vehicle has the late-type squared top edge on the glacis, with a slight protrusion above the hull roof. The main weapon is the 76 mm Gun M1A2, characterized by the presence of a muzzle brake.

"GIDEON," when photographed, was painted with replica markings for the twelfth vehicle of Company A, 191st Tank Battalion, 7th Armored Division. The tracks are the T84 type, with rubber blocks incorporating chevron grousers.

Rearview mirrors are installed on each side of the glacis of "GIDEON." On the center of the left sponson is a first-aid kit housed in an armored box, associated with postwar tanks.

Various styles of sprockets were used on the HVSS sprocket assemblies; this one is the "economy" style, which lacked the fancy cutouts around its inner perimeter. The drum of the HVSS sprocket assembly was wider than the one for the VVSS, due to the wider tracks.

The front-left bogie assembly and two of the track-support rollers, a small one with a single wheel and a larger, dual-wheel one, are depicted. The snubber, or shock absorber, is connected to the tops of the suspension arms. The suspension arms are pinned to the bottom of the bogie bracket, and the two horizontal-volute-spring units are below the snubber.

The left-rear bogie assembly, two track-return roller assemblies, and the idler wheel are displayed. Above the engine deck is the torsion bar for the left grille/door. The supports for the fender are short pieces of U-channel steel.

A close-up study of part of the left suspension shows the inner side of the T84 track, including the hollow center guides. Also seen are a single, small, track-support roller, *right*, and a larger, dual roller, *left*.

The left T84 track is viewed from a close perspective at the rear of the vehicle, including the end connectors and the connections for the center guides.

The exhaust deflector, of sheet-metal construction, is below the upper rear of the hull. On the rear of the lower hull, below the deflector, is a tow pintle, flanked by dual tow eyes.

The turret of the M4A3(76)W that was in the collections of the Ropkey Armor Museum, Crawfordsville, Indiana, is observed from the upper left. The pistol port and the loader's hatch are open. A spotlight is on the mount to the right front of the loader's periscope. A dustcover is secured with clips over the gun shield.

A spotlight is stored in its lowered position on its mounting on the turret roof. Between the loader's periscope and the cupola is a folded-down travel lock for the .50-caliber machine gun. To the left are the late-type vane sight and the gunner's periscope, to the rear of which is the cupola. To the lower left are casting marks, including the part number of the turret type with the oval hatch for the loader (for a 76 mm gun): the D7054366.

The D7054366 turret is viewed from over the front left corner, with the spotlight, the loader's periscope, the .50-caliber machine gun's travel lock, and the loader's hatch in view. The machine gun pedestal is screwed to a square pad welded to the roof to the rear of the cupola.

The cupola assembly, equipped with six glass vision blocks, is mounted on a race, allowing the entire unit to rotate freely. In addition, the hatch door consists of a hinged frame with a freely rotating dome on it. The dome contains a periscope and a grab handle; the lid for the periscope is closed here.

CHAPTER 4
The Howitzer-Armed M4A3(105)

The Sherman, from the outset, was planned as a somewhat flexible design, capable of using not only a variety of power plants, but also a variety of armament. Among those weapons was the M4 105 mm howitzer. Production of the M4 Sherman armed with the M4 105 mm howitzer began at the Chrysler-operated Detroit Tank Arsenal in February 1944. These tanks were designated M4(105). In May, production of the M4A3 armed with the M4 105 mm howitzer began at Chrysler as well. Chrysler was the sole producer of both types of 105 mm armed vehicles.

In both cases, the weapon was installed via the Combination Mount M52. The howitzer-armed tanks utilized the D78461 high-bustle turret castings with a pistol port in the left sidewall and a hatch for the loader in the left turret roof. A second ventilator fan was added to the turret rear roof above the radio in order to cope with the additional fumes from the 105 mm round. Internally,

these turrets lacked the gyrostabilizer and power traverse of 75 mm gun tanks, and only a partial turret basket was installed. As the newer D82183 cupola, the so-called vision cupola, became more abundant in the second quarter of 1944, they began to be installed on the M4A3(105) instead.

Production of the M4A3(105) began in May 1944 and continued until June 1945. During this time, a total of 2,654 of these tanks were produced. The first 500 of these were equipped with the VVSS like all the other tanks discussed to this point in the book. The final 2,154 M4A3(105) Shermans used the new HVSS described in the previous chapter. The M4A3(105) was a dry ammunition stowage tank.

The M4A3(105)s were assigned to the headquarters companies of armored units in Europe. They appear to have made their combat debut in February 1945.

The Sherman tank design lent itself well to adapting weapons other than the 75 mm and 76 mm guns to the chassis. One of those was the 105 mm howitzer. Some of these weapons were installed in Medium Tanks M4, in addition to which Chrysler completed 500 examples of the M4A3(105) with VVSS, and 2,539 M4A3(105)s with HVSS, with production spanning from May 1944 to June 1945. Shown here is a Chrysler M4A3(105) with VVSS, registration number 30103420, completed under Production Order T-9368/1. *FCA North America Archives*

The correct caption is: M4A3(105) with VVSS registration number 30111190 has its howitzer lowered on to the travel lock, and a canvas muzzle cover is strapped over the barrel. This piece was the 105mm Howitzer M4 on the Combination Gun Mount M52. This gun mount included a new rotor shield, with two lifting incorporated on the top of it. On this example, a dust cover is attached to the shield and the front of the turret. *Patton Museum*

M4A3(105) with VVSS registration number 30103622 was photographed during evaluations by the Office of the Chief of Ordnance, Detroit, on May 9, 1945. Here, the dustcover is not installed between the rotor shield and the turret. The M4A3(105) was well suited to the indirect-fire mission, as well as in laying down 105 mm artillery fire in close-range, direct-fire scenarios. *TACOM LCMC History Office*

The turret for the M4A3(105) with HVSS was a reworked D50878 turret for the 75 mm gun, with provisions for the howitzer and its combination mount. These turrets were equipped with oblong hatches for the loader. This example had the cupola, but some vehicles had the split hatch in this location. Two ventilators were installed on the roof: one in the original position on the front center of the roof, and a new one on the top center of the bustle. *Patton Museum*

In a rear view of M4A3(105)W with VVSS registration number 30103305, the rear ventilator on the top of the turret bustle has a tilted attitude, matching the slope of the bustle. Because the ventilator occupied the former position of the machine-gun pedestal mount, a bracket was devised that straddled the ventilator, and the pedestal was mounted on it. *Patton Museum*

In addition to the 500 M4A3(105)s with VVSS produced by Chrysler Tank Arsenal, that plant also completed 2,539 M4A3(105) Shermans with the horizontal-volute suspension system. This example, numbered "221" on the left mudguard, lacks a visible registration number. Note the dustcover and its fittings on the howitzer mount, and the prominent casting marks on the right side of the mantlet and the interior of the driver's hatch door. *Patton Museum*

As seen from above, M4A3(105)W with HVSS registration number 30141434 was a late-production example of this vehicle. It has torsion bars for the grille/doors, a Korean War modification, and an infantry telephone box is mounted on the right rear of the upper hull. The nickname BANG-UP is painted on the turret. *Patton Museum*

This restored M4A3(105) with HVSS was photographed at the Ropkey Armor Museum, Crawfordsville, Indiana. The vehicle bears replica USMC markings. *Skip Warvel*

To the right of the bedroll rack on the rear of the upper hull is an infantry telephone in a metal box, by which support troops could communicate securely with the tank crew. The exhaust deflector is the two-component, armored type, with two top hinges for each half of the deflector. The tracks are the T80 model. *Skip Warvel*

The baggage rack, infantry telephone box, and exhaust deflector are visible in a rear view of the M4A3(105)W with HVSS while in the collection of the Ropkey Armor Museum. With the turret traversed slightly to the left, the storage brackets for the .50-caliber machine gun are visible on the turret bustle. *Skip Warvel*

As seen in a left-rear view, the fenders of the M4A3(105)W with HVSS had turned-down outer edges with holes in them for screwing on the sand shields. Toward the forward end of the left sponson is an armored first-aid kit.

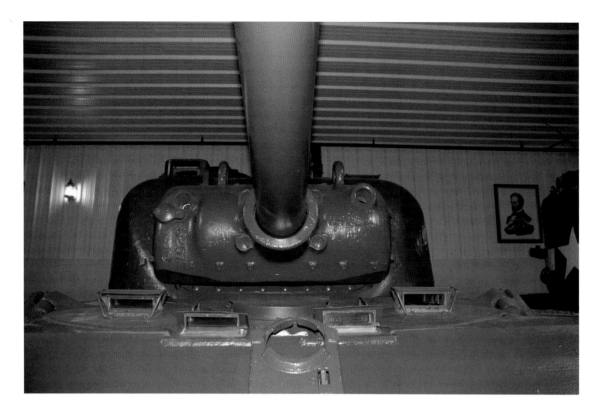

The rotor shield of the M4A3(105) with HVSS is viewed from the front. On the right side of the shield is the aperture for the gunner's direct sight, with a pivoting cover, shown in the open position. Below that port are vertically oriented casting marks. On the left side of the shield is the port for the coaxial Browning M199A4 .30-caliber machine gun. In the foreground are the driver's and assistant driver's rotating-hatch periscopes and fixed periscopes; to the rear of the fixed periscopes is the ventilator hood.

The turret is viewed from the upper left, with the loader's hatch open and the pistol port ajar. Note the bracket for the machine gun pedestal on the turret roof, which straddles the ventilator.

The left front of the M4A3(105) with HVSS at the Ropkey Armor Museum is seen from above. The sides of the gun shield, between the turret and the rotor shield or mantlet, are semicircular; actually, slightly larger than a half circle. On the hull roof to the side of the driver's hatch are casting marks. Square bosses tapped for screws are welded to the rotor shield and the turret, for attaching a dustcover.

The gun shield and the rotor shield of the Ropkey Armor Museum's M4A3(105) with HVSS are observed from the right side. Below the howitzer barrel and the center of the rotor shield, the ventilator hood, with its low profile, is in view between the drivers' hatches.

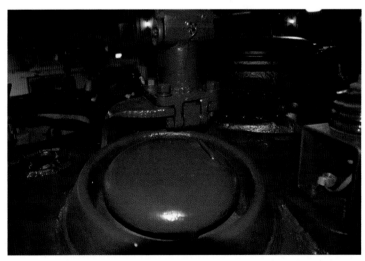

The bracket straddling the rear roof vent, which supports the pedestal for the .50-caliber machine gun, is viewed from the front left. To the left, on the roof, is the trademark of the manufacturer of the turret, a letter *G* inside an octagon, representing American Steel Foundries, Granite City, Illinois.

As seen from the rear, the machine gun pedestal is attached to the bracket with a hinge, so that the bracket can be lowered during travel. When in the raised position, the pedestal was secured to the bracket with four hex screws.

CHAPTER 5
Heavyweight Sherman: The M4A3E2

Ordnance developed the M4A3E2 in anticipation of a need for an assault tank to back up the infantry during the upcoming invasion of France. With slight modifications, it was discovered, the new M4A3 with the 47-degree hull could bear significantly increased armor protection.

Initially, an additional 2 inches of armor were welded over the standard 47-degree glacis plate, and side armor was increased with an addition of 1½-inch armor plates. As a result, the thickness of the glacis became 4 inches, while side armor was 3 inches thick. A new casting up to 5½ inches thick replaced the differential/final-drive cover. A new turret was introduced, one based on the form of the 76 mm turret that had been worked out as part of the T23 program, except that the pistol port was deleted from the left sidewall. The armor of the massive casting was 6 inches thick on the sides, while the rear thickness was 2½ inches. The roof plate was welded on.

Under the original conception of an infantry support tank, the M3 75 mm gun would be fitted into a mount based on the M62 mount that served on 76 mm turrets. By adding more plate to the outside of the standard 76 mm part, the 7-inch-thick outer gun shield was produced.

In an effort to increase the life of the power train, the final-drive ratio was increased—the only automotive change in the vehicle. As a result of this modification, however, the tank's top speed was reduced to about 22 mph. The tracks of all these tanks had extended end connectors, a feature designed to reduce ground pressure from the vehicles' 84,000-pound weight. This great weight also put excessive burden on the tanks' standard VVSS suspension. Photographs of the vehicles from the time frequently show a variety of road wheels, attesting to the need for replacements due to the failure of bearings and to compressed suspensions.

Beginning in May, a total of 254 of the M4A3E2s were manufactured by Fisher Tank Arsenal under production order T-9724.

M4A3E2 tanks began to show up in Europe shortly after D-Day in June 1944. Massive in size, the tank, dubbed the "Jumbo," was able to withstand punishment from German gunfire. Many of the M4A3E2s were later regunned with the 76 mm—a conversion facilitated by the fact that the tank already incorporated the gun mount based on the M62. Though not present in large numbers, M4A3E2 tanks were popular point tanks in US armored detachments until VE-Day.

The M4A3E2 "Jumbo" represented an effort to up-armor the basic M4A3 to improve its survivability during combat assaults. Fisher Tank Arsenal completed 254 of these vehicles. The hulls were converted from existing M4A3 hulls by adding an additional 2-inch-thick armor plate over the glacis, installing extra 1-inch armor plates to the sides of the sponsons, and replacing the original final-drive assembly with an armor housing up to 5½ inches thick. The turret was similar to the turret for the 76 mm gun but with 6-inch side armor and a new mantlet, and armed with a 75 mm Gun M3. Pictured here is the first production MA3E2, registration number 3082923 and Ordnance number 50326. *FCA North America Archives*

A Medium Tank M4A3E2, registration number 3082923, is viewed from the right side during testing on June 5, 1944. A vertical weld joint existed on the side of the sponson armor above the center bogie bracket. The 75 mm Gun M3 was in a modified Combination Gun Mount M62, as used in the 76 mm Gun M4A3, and was redesignated for the M4A3E2 as the Combination Gun Mount T110. This gun mount included a greatly modified gun shield, in which the original 2-inch armor received an extra layer of 5-inch armor. *Patton Museum*

As seen in a right-rear view of M4A3E2 with registration number 3082923, "duckbill" extended end connectors generally were installed on the tracks, to improve flotation of the heavy vehicle, but sometimes these were absent in actual practice. The T48 tracks were on this tank. The contours of the turret's right side and bustle, which included an armored hood for the ventilator, are visible. *Patton Museum*

The additional armor on the turret and the upper hull is in view in this elevated photo of M4A3E2 with registration number 3082923 on June 5, 1944. The joint between the original turret top and the top of the additional armor is particularly visible from the gunner's periscope to the outer part of the cupola, and from the cupola to the outboard side of the antenna bracket to the rear of the cupola. *Patton Museum*

The first production M4A3E2, registration number 3082923 and Ordnance number 50326, is seen from the upper right at Aberdeen Proving Ground on August 23, 1944. Between this date and June 5, 1944, when the preceding photos of this tank were taken, several modifications had been made to the tank. Sand skirts were screwed to extension strips that were tack-welded to the sponsons; these extensions provided clearance between the duckbill end connectors, when installed on the tracks, and the sand skirts. In addition, there were several new, vertical weld beads on the armor plate on the side of the sponson. These beads do not extend all the way to the top of the armor and may have been an experiment to further bond the added-on armor to the original armor of the sponson. *Patton Museum*

The rear mud flaps of the first production M4A3E2, as seen at Aberdeen on August 23, 1944, were extra wide, to allow for the extra width of the tracks when duckbill end connectors were installed. *Patton Museum*

An M4A3E2 under testing by the Armored Force Board at Fort Knox, Kentucky, has a dustcover snapped into place over the mount for the bow machine gun. The brackets on which the bottoms of the travel lock pivoted were higher off the glacis than on other models of the Sherman. The barrel of the 75 mm gun entered the gun shield through a cylindrical housing, slightly above the center of the housing. Pressed Steel Car Company built, under subcontract, the turrets and gun mounts for the M4A3E2. Headlights and siren were not part of the equipment of the M4A3E2. *Patton Museum*

The same M4A3E2 is seen from the left side during testing by the Armored Force Board Test Operation. The extra weight of the additional armor on this vehicle put enormous stresses on the suspension. In particular, crews were instructed to avoid situations that would cause shocks to the front bogies, since their vertical volute springs were found to break under such circumstances.

During analysis of an M4A3E2 by the Ordnance Operation, Engineering Standards Vehicle Laboratory, Detroit, on August 3, 1944, a worker is taking measurements of clearances between the recoil shield of the 75 mm Gun M3 and the ceiling of the turret. The photo was taken from the left side of the turret. Worthy of notice are the lateral weld beads on the turret roof to each side of the loader's hatch. *Patton Museum*

This series of photos was taken in the fighting compartment of the first production M4A3E2, registration number 3082925, with the turret and turret basket removed, on June 5, 1944. Here, 75 mm rounds are arranged vertically in bins in the foreground. Farther forward are the driver's seat and controls, the transmission (with four periscopes and six spare periscope heads stored above it), and the assistant driver's seat and the mount for the bow machine gun. *Patton Museum*

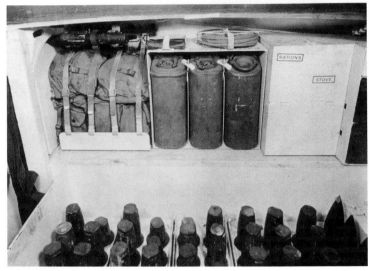

Stowage in the right sponson included, *left to right*, an M3 .45-caliber submachine gun over crew packs, a collapsible canvas bucket atop a bin containing three 5-gallon liquid containers for water, and a metal box containing rations and a field stove. *Patton Museum*

The left sponson contains, *left to right*, the auxiliary generator, a bin for six 2-inch smoke-mortar rounds, and machine-gun ammunition boxes. To the right is a case for a signal gun and flares. To the lower left are the two fixed fire extinguishers. On the bottom are 75 mm ammunition rounds. *Patton Museum*

The turret of the M4A3E2 is viewed from the rear of the 75 mm gun. On the ceiling are, *left to right*, the loader's periscope, the interior travel lock for the gun mount, and a dome light. To the lower left, a .50-caliber machine gun has been installed in the coaxial mount. To the right of that gun is the gyrostabilizer cylinder. At the center is the recoil and carriage assembly of the gun mount, with an elevation quadrant attached to the top of it. To the right are the gunner's direct sight and a link rod to the gunner's periscope. *Patton Museum*

Medium Tank M4A3E2 with registration number 3082928 is one of a handful of surviving Jumbos. When photographed, it lacked the duckbill end connectors on the tracks and was equipped with solid-spoked bogie wheels and idler wheels. *Chris Hughes*

The raised brackets for the travel lock, the design of the gun shield, and the lines of the hull armor joints are presented in this photo. Between the hatches are the lids for two fixed periscopes and the ventilator. Note the muzzle of the 2-inch smoke mortar protruding from the left front of the turret roof. *Chris Hughes*

The right side of the gun shield of the M4A3E2 is displayed, showing the weld seam between the original gun shield and the added-on armor. A cutout in the side of the shield permits access to the trunnion plate. Note the casting number, "111," to the left. *Chris Hughes*

The gun shield is viewed from the upper right, showing the various weld seams and facets of the armor. *Chris Hughes*

The gun shield is observed from the front, illustrating the nonconcentric position of the 75 mm gun barrel in the cylindrical projection on the front of the shield. A groove is scored around the opening for the gun barrel on the front of that cylinder. *Chris Hughes*

The lower part of the gun shield, the ventilator, the travel lock and its hold-down latch and raised mounting brackets, and the bow machine gun are in view. *Chris Hughes*

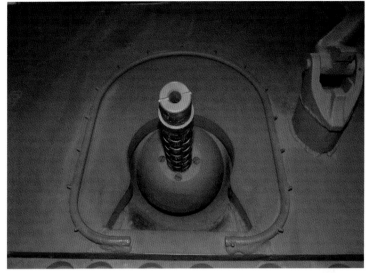

The top armor of the glacis had a keyhole-shaped cut in it to allow clearance for the ball mount of the machine gun. Around the bow machine gun is welded a bent tube with snap fittings for attaching a dustcover. *Chris Hughes*

The final-drive assembly of the M4A3E2 had thickened armor, in keeping with the up-armored nature of the vehicle. On the left side of the unit is a clamp for securing a tow cable. Lower down are dual tow eyes with welded-on steps. *Chris Hughes*

The turret roof of the M4A3E2 presented a flat surface. The joint between the supplemental armor and the turret roof is clearly visible in the right foreground and toward the rear of the turret. In the foreground, the loader's periscope has been removed. On the right rear of the roof is a base for a radio antenna. *Chris Hughes*

CHAPTER 6
Double-Barrel Sherman: The POA-CWS-H5

It comes as no surprise that flame has been weaponized. Flame not only inspires the fear of being directly burned, but it also threatens to detonate nearby munitions. In addition, even when personnel are not directly targeted, flamethrowers can superheat the air and cut off life-giving oxygen. In the Pacific theater, flame weapons proved particularly useful for just these reasons. The CWS-POA-H5 represented the pinnacle of US flamethrower development in the Second World War. A formidable weapon system, the CWS-POA-H5 combined the conventional punch of the Sherman's main gun with the advantages of a powerful flamethrower. In addition, much of the Sherman's secondary machine-gun armament was retained.

In anticipation of the planned invasion of the Japanese home islands, the Pacific Ocean Area–Chemical Warfare Service in Hawaii converted seventy of the 75 mm and 105 mm armed Sherman tanks to the CWS-POA-H5 configuration. These tanks incorporated the M5-4 (E12-7R1) mechanized flamethrower, a weapon that had been engineered by Standard Oil Development Company. With a range of 100 yards, the flamethrower weapon carried 290 gallons of fuel, allowing for two full minutes of flame or 200 bursts of one second each.

Stowage of ammunition for conventional weapons was reduced aboard the CWS-POA-H5 to make room for the flame unit. As a result, only forty rounds of 75 mm ammunition or twenty rounds of 105 mm ammunition could be carried in the vehicle.

Formidable though the CWS-POA-H5 was, the tanks were not employed for their intended purpose during World War II. They remained in storage and served in training until the Korean War broke out in June 1950. Three of the tanks landed in Korea on September 15, 1950, and took part in the liberation of Seoul. In the end, nine M4A3(105) with HVSS tanks fitted with the M5-4 flame system deployed to Korea to serve as the Flame Platoon, Headquarters Company, 1st Tank Battalion, 1st Marine Division, Fleet Marine Force. The vehicles were heavily involved in combat and proved highly effective.

Sherman tanks were used as platforms for flamethrowers. This example was an M4A3(105) CWS-POA-H5 with HVSS, armed with an M5-4 (E12-7R1) mechanized flamethrower to the right of the 105 mm howitzer. The Standard Oil Development Company developed this flamethrower, which had a range of 100 yards. This tank is seen during tests of the flamethrower on Oahu on July 15, 1945. *National Archives*

Shown here is a line of four flame tanks performing a demonstration on Oahu on April 26, 1945. The nearest one, which is firing napalm, is an M4 Composite. The other three tanks are large-hatch vehicles with 75 mm guns, possibly M4A3s. *National Archives*

A US Marine Corps large-hatch M4A3(75) CWS-POA-H5 tank with VVSS, equipped with a Bulldozer M1, is undergoing testing at Quantico, Virginia, on July 27, 1950. The USMC serial number of this flame tank is 102234. *USMC*

The same USMC M4A3(75) CWS-POA-H5 flamethrower tank shown in the preceding photo is laying down flame at a range at Quantico, Virginia, on July 27, 1945. The dozer blade, present in the preceding view, has been removed. *USMC*

During Army maneuvers in Tennessee in January 1944, a crewman of a small-hatch, dry-stowage M4A3 is performing maintenance on the engine. Toolboxes and engine parts, including camshafts and, *to the right*, a camshaft housing, are in evidence. Note the bulky traps on the insides of the grille/doors, designed to prevent foreign objects that infiltrated the grilles from coming to rest on the engine. *Mike Haines collection*

Mechanics are maneuvering a new-appearing Ford GAA engine above the engine compartment of an M4A3 during the January 1944 Tennessee maneuvers. The man to the left has his right hand on the right magneto. Note the continuous pad on the bottom of the lifting eye on the sponson.
Mike Haines collection

Three reddish rings with white borders are painted on the barrel of the 76 mm Gun M1A1C of a Medium Tank M4A3(76)W from the 1st Tank Battalion, 1st Armored Division, operating outside Pauglia, Italy, on September 1, 1944. The recognition stars have received, apparently, a thinned coat of Olive Drab paint, to make them less of a target. A moisture-crumpled sheet of paper, apparently a magazine illustration, but not of the pinup-art type, has been taped to the front of the star on the sponson. The purpose of the T-shaped object to the side of the vane sight is not clear. *National Archives*

In a photograph dated September 7, 1944, two GIs from the 1st Armored Division are completing a telephone-line communication between an M4A3(76)W, with an outlined number "2" on the turret, and a headquarters unit, somewhere in Italy. The recognition star on the turret is faint and irregular, probably as a result of being painted over to reduce its visibility. *National Archives*

A large-hatch M4A3(75) assigned to the 737th Tank Battalion approaches the outskirts of Nancy, France, on September 15, 1944. The turret has a split hatch on the right side of the roof and a loader's hatch, which is ajar, on the left side. *National Archives*

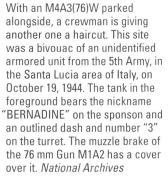

With an M4A3(76)W parked alongside, a crewman is giving another one a haircut. This site was a bivouac of an unidentified armored unit from the 5th Army, in the Santa Lucia area of Italy, on October 19, 1944. The tank in the foreground bears the nickname "BERNADINE" on the sponson and an outlined dash and number "3" on the turret. The muzzle brake of the 76 mm Gun M1A2 has a cover over it. *National Archives*

After the capture of Cherbourg, France, in late June 1944, that city became an important port of entry for American war materiel for the push across Europe. Here, newly arrived Sherman medium tanks are being prepared for transport to the fighting front, including, *at the center*, an M4A3(105) with VVSS. The large crate on its engine deck contained spare parts and equipment removed from the tank for shipment. Shipping stencils and chalk marks are on the sponson and final-drive assembly. *National Archives*

At the Port of Cherbourg, France, newly arrived US Army Sherman tanks and other armored vehicles are being prepared for transit to the front lines, on November 4, 1944. In the foreground is an M4A3E2 Jumbo. The turret's serial number, "100," is near the front of its right side. In the background are small-hatch and large-hatch Shermans and a Tank Recovery Vehicle M32. *National Archives*

Soldiers are surveying a complex tank-recovery problem: a 6th Armored Division M4A3E2 that has come to rest on its right side on a creek bed at St.-Jean-Rohrbach, France, on November 26, 1944. Duckbill end connectors are installed on the outside of the T48 tracks. *National Archives*

A column of tanks, including several large-hatch M4A3(75)s, is advancing through the village of Ciery, France, in November 1944. The two closest vehicles are using the spare-track racks on their right rears for liquid-container racks. The nearest tank has a US 5-gallon can on the rack, while the next vehicle has a German Jerry can. Browning M2HB .50-caliber machine guns are stored, with barrels installed and canvas covers over them, on the rears of the bustles of the closest two Shermans. *National Archives*

During the advance into Langerwehe, Germany, on November 26, 1944, an M4A3E2 navigates a flooded street, with a bombed-out railroad bridge in the background. A tow cable is wound around the travel lock on the glacis. Duckbill end connectors are installed on the tracks. *National Archives*

A large-hatch, wet-stowage M4A3(75), registration number 3081592, from the 23rd Tank Battalion, 12th Armored Division, fell into this predicament when it backed into an existing bomb crater when suddenly faced by a German antitank gun near Guising, France, on December 15, 1944. This tank was completed by Fisher Tank Arsenal in March 1944. The nickname "BUCKLAND BEAUTY" is present on the sponson. Casting marks on the turret bustle indicate it was manufactured by Pittsburgh Steel Foundry in January 1944. On the embankment to the right of center, GIs are inspecting the wreckage of a turretless large-hatch Sherman hull, lying on its left side. On the embankment toward the left are two M32 tank-recovery vehicles and a 76 mm Sherman. *National Archives*

Crewmen of an M4A3(76)W with serial number 30100110 are brushing whitewash on their tank as a winter camouflage measure in December 1944. The man on the left is brushing snow off the bow machine gun mount with a broom. This tank was completed at the Chrysler Tank Arsenal in May 1944. *National Archives*

An M4A3(76)W of the 3rd Armored Division rolls past its nemesis, a knocked-out Panther tank, on a forest trail outside Bovigny, Belgium, on January 17, 1945. Below the board for retaining the sandbags on the glacis is the lower part of a large recognition star enclosed in a circle. Evergreen boughs have been arranged on the tank for camouflage, and, as a modification, a .50-caliber machine gun on a pedestal mount is to the front of the loader's hatch. *National Archives*

Two 7th US Army Shermans with sandbag armor on the glacises, including an M4A3(76)W at the front and a 75 mm-armed vehicle to the rear, have taken position on a street in the bombed-out village of Surbourg, France, on January 19, 1945. The tanks are heavily camouflaged with evergreen boughs, netting, and, on the side of the turret of the closer tank, British-type scrim net. *National Archives*

An M4A3E2, freshly camouflaged for winter conditions with whitewash, is parked in a doorway in an unidentified town on January 20, 1945. Even the dustcover for the bow machine gun has been whitewashed, but the interior of the driver's hatch retains its original Olive Drab paint. *Patton Museum*

A photographer encountered these two whitewashed M4A3(105)s with VVSS in the vicinity of Hochdelden, France, toward the end of January 1945. Sandbags are stacked on the glacis of both vehicles, and a white-and-red-striped aiming stake, used for setting up a howitzer for indirect fire, is on the top edge of the sponson next to the turret of the lead tank. *National Archives*

Using a winch cable from a half-track, crewmen of a large-hatch M4A3(75) attached to the 735th Tank Battalion are performing a change of tracks in the vicinity of Wiltz, Luxembourg, on January 26, 1945. The tank has a camouflage treatment of whitewash, with areas of Olive Drab paint showing as well. A storage rail made from a welded rod has been attached to the turret, to carry crew packs. The auxiliary generator in the tank is running, as evidenced by the smoke emanating from the exhaust pipe under the left sponson. *National Archives*

Sherman tanks were not well protected against German antitank guns, and in the later stages of the war the dreaded *Panzerfaust*, a handheld, recoilless antitank weapon that fired a shaped-charge projectile capable of cutting through the thickest of armor, posed an enhanced threat. Thus, tank units often took measures in the field to increase the Shermans' protection, including installing additional armor or track sections or piling sandbags on the sides and fronts of the hulls and the sides of the turrets. This M4A3 from the 25th Tank Battalion, 14th Armored Division, US 7th Army, photographed in France on February 11, 1945, has the so-called sandbag armor on the glacis and the sides of the sponsons. The sandbags are secured to the sponsons with locally fabricated metal racks. The sandbags on the glacis are simply piled on, with a piece of lumber at the bottom to retain them. *National Archives*

Unit markings on US Army Shermans of World War II are often difficult to read or are not visible in photos. On this M4A3(76) W with HVSS, on the other hand, the markings are in plain view on the 76 mm gun barrel: they represent vehicle number "6," Company C, 25th Tank Battalion, 14th Armored Division. This tank has, in addition to the typical crosspiece on the final-drive assembly for retaining sandbag armor, an extra frame with a vertical support in the center, to help keep the sandbags firmly on the glacis. Also, well-constructed metal racks for holding sandbags on the sides of the sponson have been welded on but have not yet been filled with sandbags. *National Archives*

Outside Saarburg, Germany, on February 14, 1945, troops and vehicles of the 10th Armored Division, US 3rd Army, including a large-hatch M4A3(75) in the foreground, await orders to proceed to a pontoon bridge being constructed across the Saar River. A split hatch is present on the turret; on the side of the turret is a rail for stowing crew knapsacks. Slung over the front end of the 75 mm gun barrel is the sling of a .45-caliber "Grease Gun" submachine gun. A collapsible canvas bucket is secured to the right brush guard. *National Archives*

A large-hatch M4A3(75) from the 10th Armored Division stands watch in Adolf Hitler Platz, in Trier, Germany, around the end of the battle for that city on March 2, 1945. A 5-gallon liquid container is on the engine deck, and crates and baggage covered by a tarpaulin are on the rear of the hull. Duckbill end connectors are on the tracks. *National Archives*

Members of the 730th Tank Battalion, 83rd Division, 9th Army, are removing 105 mm ammunition from fiberboard packing tubes in order to replenish an M4A3(105) with HVSS during the advance to Düsseldorf, Germany, on March 3, 1945. A log across the bow serves as a retainer for the sandbags on the glacis, while a frame made of bits of lumber and wire holds sandbags on the side of the sponson. *National Archives*

The crew of an M4A3E2 Jumbo look intently to the front as they pass through a town near Koblenz, Germany, on March 9, 1945. This is one of the Jumbos that was armed with a 76 mm gun; on this tank it is the 76 mm Gun M1A1C, with a cuff screwed onto the threaded end of the barrel. The travel lock is not the long, 76 mm gun type, but rather a modified 75 mm gun type with extensions to make it taller than the stock item. Chicken wire is rigged to the turret, the glacis, and the sponsons for attaching tree branches for camouflage. Modified mounts are present for a Browning .30-caliber machine gun on the cupola and a Browning .50-caliber machine gun to the front of the loader's hatch. *Patton Museum*

Sherman medium tanks from the 23rd Tank Battalion, XXI Corps, US 7th Army, have pulled over into a field in order to await orders for their positions for the advance to Lauterbach, Germany, on March 13, 1945. Except for the 76 mm Sherman with VVSS to the right, the tanks are M4A3(76)W with HVSS, one of which, the second tank from the right, has sandbag armor on the hull. *National Archives*

An M4A3E2 from the 4th Armored Division rolls through the town of Alzey, Germany, on March 20, 1945. The Jumbo has been given the chicken-wire treatment, for rigging tree branches, on the glacis, sponson, and turret side. The main weapon is a 76 mm Gun M1A1, and the travel lock is the type used on Shermans armed with the 76 mm gun. The weapons on the turret roof are a .30-caliber machine gun to the front of the cupola and a pedestal-mounted .50-caliber machine gun to the front of the loader's hatch. *National Archives*

The crew of a 4th Armored Division M4A3E2 armed with a 76 mm Gun M1A1 enjoy a break while an M4A3(76)W with HVSS moves up to the right, during the capture of Alzey, Germany, on March 20, 1945. Markings on the final-drive assembly of the M4A3(76)W with HVSS are for the first vehicle of Headquarters Company, 37th Tank Battalion, 4th Armored Division. The tracks on that vehicle are the T66 type. *National Archives*

An M4A3E2 Jumbo armed with a 76 mm Gun M1A1 leads the way as a column of 4th Armored Division tanks strikes deep into Germany on March 20, 1945. Abandoned and burning German vehicles are along the side of the road. The second tank in line, which is, unfortunately, obscured by road dust, is an M4A3(76)W with HVSS with additional armor plate on the front of the final-drive assembly and on the sides of the turret. *National Archives*

The commander and the loader of this M4A3(76)W are not gazing at the photographer but rather are looking at the bodies of a *Panzerfaust* team, killed along the road, on March 27, 1945. The main gun is the 76 mm M1A1C, with the screw-on muzzle sleeve. *National Archives*

A German infantryman firing a *Panzerfaust* or a *Panzerschreck* (bazooka) knocked out this 6th Armored Division M4A3(76)W on March 27, 1945. The rubber blocks of the right track have burned off, baggage stored on the rear of the vehicle is in ashes, and the vehicle is still smoking. *Patton Museum*

"Doughs," as tankers liked to call infantrymen, hitch a ride on a large-hatch M4A3 from the 17th Tank Battalion, 7th Armored Division, during the march into Wetzlar, Germany, on March 28, 1945. This tank has a sheet-metal exhaust deflector. Extra-long, and possibly locally made, duckbill end connectors are on the T54E1 tracks. The rear mudguards are missing. *National Archives*

A large-hatch Sherman with a 75 mm gun and the nickname "AIM" painted on the sponson, in the foreground, and an M4A3(76) W with HVSS, registration number 3032323, from the 8th Armored Division, 9th US Army, are dueling with German artillery outside Kirschhellen, Germany, in late March 1945. The HVSS Sherman was completed at the Chrysler Defense Arsenal in November 1944. *National Archives*

The attention of members of the crew of a 7th Armored Division M4A3(76)W has been drawn to something occurring to their right, as the vehicle passes a sign for Haina, Germany, on March 30, 1945. The nickname "MINNESOTA KID" is painted on the glacis in front of the driver's hatch. Duckbill end connectors are on the tracks; one in missing on the front of the right track. Coming around the bend in the background is an M4A3(76)W with HVSS. *National Archives*

Sherman tanks and, to the far right, a Tank Recovery Vehicle M32, from the 9th Armored Division, 1st US Army, are awaiting orders to advance after being refueled in a field at Westhousen, Germany, on April 10, 1945. As far as is discernible, all of the Shermans are large-hatch, wet-stowage M4A3(75)s. On the closest tank, the front lifting rings are near the edge of the glacis: a late-production practice at Fisher Tank Arsenal. *National Archives*

A late-production large-hatch M4A3(75) attached to Combat Command B, 7th Armored Division, 1st US Army, pauses next to a dead Waffen-SS soldier in Oberkirchen, Germany, on or around April 5, 1945. Steel rods have been welded to the sponson and the turret to hold on chicken wire, for attaching branches for camouflage. A steel I beam serves as a retainer for the spare bogie wheels and sandbags on the glacis. By now, it was common practice to lash logs to the sides of the upper hulls of Sherman tanks for added protection against shaped-charge antitank projectiles. *National Archives*

The 30th Infantry Division "Old Hickory" captured the city of Braunschweiger, Germany, on April 10, 1945. On that occasion, a GI is hunkered down across the street from an M4A3(76)W with HVSS. The sheet-metal exhaust deflector has taken a beating in service. The loader's split-hatch doors, *left*, and the commander's cupola hatch, *right*, are open. An unusual touch is the storage of spare track links horizontally on the rear of the upper hull. *National Archives*

An M4A3(76)W with HVSS, from the 21st Tank Battalion, Combat Command A, 10th Armored Division, is serving as a battle taxi for doughs during the advance toward Bubenorbis, Germany, in mid-April 1945. Stencils with shipping and administrative information are plentiful on the side of the sponson. *National Archives*

In a photo datelined April 16, 1945, a column of Sherman tanks from Company B, 43rd Tank Battalion, Combat Command A, 12th Armored Division, have paused along a pine forest during the advance to Nuremberg. The first four tanks are M4A3(76)Ws with HVSS and are equipped with T80 tracks, which saw limited use at the very end of the war in Europe, the T66 tracks being far more common on HVSS vehicles in World War II. The last three Shermans in the line are an M4A3(76)W, a 75 mm Sherman, and another M4A3(76)W. *National Archives*

Having broken a wooden bridge not meant for armored vehicles, an M4A3(76)W with HVSS is struggling to extricate itself. The site was near Dietersheim, Germany, on April 14, 1945, and the unit was Company A, 714th Tank Battalion, Combat Command B, 12th Armored Division. On the sponson of this vehicle is a tactical sign of a letter *A* over a chevron, which is over a square dot. The first tank in the background is a small-hatch, dry-stowage Sherman with a 75 mm gun. *National Archives*

An M4A3(76)W with the 5th US Army is passing over very rough ground on a ridge in the Monterumici area of Italy on April 17, 1945. Duckbill end connectors are installed on the steel tracks. Instead of retaining sandbags, a board across the bow serves to hold several boxes in place. After this Sherman recovered from its predicament, engineers erected a treadway bridge over the stream. *National Archives*

On April 26, 1945, an M4A3(76)W with VVSS is advancing through a village in the Po River valley in Italy. A placard that appears to be a bent license plate is hanging from the travel lock. As a field modification, racks for storing grousers have been welded to the side of the turret. Duckbill end connectors are present on the tracks. The main weapon is the 76 mm Gun M1A2, with its muzzle brake swaddled in a dustcover. *National Archives*

US Army large-hatch M4A3s saw service in the Okinawa Campaign in 1945. The crew of this 75 mm vehicle, nicknamed "CHUCK-A-LUCK," the thirteenth vehicle of Company C, 193rd Tank Battalion, is prepared to resume the advance on Kakazu Ridge on April 27, 1945. Once that ridge was secured, tanks had free rein to operate in the open country beyond. Grousers are secured to racks across the final-drive assembly. The number "55" is painted on the turret. Note the oversized appliqué armor plates on the sponson. In the background is an M7 Priest. *National Archives*

Doughs of the 328th Infantry Regiment, 26th "Yankee" Infantry Division, are catching a ride on an M4A3(76)W with VVSS outside Deggendorf, Bavaria, near the end of April 1945. These troops were mopping up the final Nazi resistance in the area. *National Archives*

Disarmed Axis soldiers are proceeding between three US Army Shermans at a border checkpoint between Italy and Austria at Brenner Pass on May 4, 1945. The front tank across the road is an M4A3(76)W with HVSS, while to its rear is a 75 mm Sherman with VVSS. To the right, a close view is offered of the T66 track. *National Archives*

The same three tanks shown in the preceding photo are viewed from the front from ground level. The tank to the left is revealed here to be an M4A3(76)W with HVSS. The two HVSS tanks have racks for sandbag armor fabricated from welded rods, while the VVSS vehicle has sandbag racks made of slats of some sort. *National Archives*

An infantryman jogs alongside an M4A3(76)W with HVSS during the advance to Innsbruck, Austria, on May 3, 1945. Very well built racks for sandbag armor have been welded onto the sponsons on the turret. The tracks are the T66 model. *National Archives*

Five Marine Corps Shermans, believed to have been remanufactured small-hatch, dry-stowage M4A3(75)s, are being prepared for a mission. Each vehicle has a bundle of logs lashed to the glacis with ropes; in several cases the logs are stacked much higher than the driver's hatch, and the turrets are turned to the rear. It is supposed that the logs were to be released in ditches or impassable obstacles to enable the vehicles to move forward. The nearest tank is a small-hatch, direct-vision one, as indicated by the presence of drivers' hoods without fixed periscopes. Steel tracks with chevron grousers (some with duckbill connectors installed) are attached to the sponsons and turret, and three I beams are attached to the bogie assemblies for further protection. *USMC*

Marines are loading field-kitchen equipment and supplies onto a remanufactured small-hatch, dry-stowage M4A3, for transport over muddy roads on Okinawa in June 1945. This is an early Ford M4A3, as indicated by the lifting eyes with pads on the bottoms and the lack of attachment strips for sand shields. *USMC*

An early-production, remanufactured, small-hatch, dry-stowage M4A3 in Marine Corps service is being loaded with field rations boxes on Okinawa in June 1945. The bogie wheels are the open-spoke type with plugs welded into the openings, to thwart daredevil Japanese soldiers from jamming steel bars in the openings to disable the running gear. *Patton Museum*

A Marine welder is fastening steel tracks with duckbill connectors attached to the bow of a small-hatch, direct-vision M4A3 on Okinawa in June 1945. The tracks installed on the suspension of the tank are the T48s, with rubber blocks with chevron grousers molded in. The remanufactured tank has appliqué armor on the fronts of the drivers' hoods. *USMC*

In August 1945, a large number of Shermans are parked at an ordnance depot in Manila, in reserve for the invasion of Japan that was anticipated before the atomic bombings of Hiroshima and Nagasaki induced the Japanese to surrender. Many of these vehicles are Fisher-produced large-hatch, wet-stowage M4A3(75)s with HVSS. The tanks still have all or much of the sealant materials that were applied before they were shipped overseas; note the sealant on the gun shields of the vehicles in the right foreground, for example. The objects stacked on the engine decks include spare-parts boxes and sections of sand shields and mudguards. *National Archives*

At the end of World War II, large numbers of US Sherman tanks were placed in storage as production of the M26 Pershing tank proceeded. When the Korean War erupted in 1950, there was again a call for Shermans. To bring them up to current combat standards, there was a series of modifications, performed at various Ordnance depots. Photographed on September 20, 1950, at the Tokyo Ordnance Center, this is an M4A3E4, a conversion of the M4A3(75) with VVSS in which the 75 mm gun was replaced by a 76 mm piece, retaining the 75 mm turret and mantlet. This vehicle has received fresh paint and modifications, including racks for spare bogie wheels and sprockets. *National Archives*

This USMC flamethrower M4A3(105) CWS-POA-H5 with HVSS, serial number 102866, armed with an M5-4 (E12-7R1) mechanized flamethrower to the right of the 105 mm howitzer, served with the 1st Marine Division and is shown in Yong Dung Po, Korea. Note the plumbing for the flamethrower alongside and above the sponson. *Patton Museum*

An M4A3(105) CWS-POA-H5 with HVSS, equipped with an M5-4 (E12-7R1) flamethrower to the right of the 105 mm howitzer, pauses next to a field tent in the vicinity of Hongchon, Korea, on March 18, 1951. A rack has been fabricated on the fender for three 5-gallon liquid containers and some ammunition boxes. *National Archives*

Tankers from Company C, 89th Tank Battalion, 25th Infantry Division, are conferring to the front of a Medium Tank M4A3(76) W with HVSS before a mission in Korea on March 6, 1951. This battalion was nicknamed "Rice's Red Devils" after its commander, Capt. Clifford Rice, and in keeping with its sobriquet, the unit painted red devil's faces on the bows of its Shermans. *National Archives*

Capt. Clifford Rice, *left*, commanding officer of the 89th Tank Battalion, and 1Lt. Fred Wilkins are making final plans for a mission somewhere in Korea on March 6, 1951. On the adjacent M4A3(76)W with HVSS, note the "LIFT HERE" stencil next to the lifting ring, and the Browning M1919A4 .30-caliber machine gun on a tripod atop the turret. *National Archives*

The nickname "RICE'S RED DEVILS" is painted on the turret of this M4A3(76)W with HVSS from Company C, 89th Tank Battalion, on the north side of the Han River in the Uchonni area of Korea on March 7, 1951. This tank was marked as the fourth vehicle of Company C. Two white recognition stars are visible on the side of the sponson, including one, partially in shadow, above the second spare track block. *National Archives*

Employing the A-frame boom of a Tank Recovery Vehicle M32 with the nickname "BRINGUM BACK" painted on the superstructure and the sponson, members of the 725th Ordnance Depot, 26th Infantry Division, are lowering the turret onto the chassis of a Medium Tank M4A3(76)W with HVSS, at Sumon, Korea, on May 4, 1951. The 76 mm gun turrets had half floors on the turret baskets, to enable the loader to better access ammunition below the basket. Visible in the basket is the gunner's seat pedestal, to the front of which is the hydraulic traversing mechanism. *National Archives*

Toward the eastern end of the fighting front in Korea in January 1952, a USMC M4A3(105) CWS-POA-H5 with HVSS has just laid down flame on a bunker abandoned by the enemy, in order to deny its use to the Communists should they reoccupy the area. The marking on the side of the turret is not all legible but appears to be F31. *US Army Chemical Corps Museum*

In a photo related to the preceding one, a Marine Corps M4A3(105) CWS-POA-H5 with HVSS is shooting flaming, jellied napalm at an abandoned enemy bunker. A spool of wire is in the rack on the forward part of the fender. *US Army Chemical Corps Museum*

A few months after the ceasefire in the Korean War, the crew of an M4A3(76)W with HVSS, assigned to the 2nd Infantry Division, are conducting a training exercise in the Republic of Korea on February 15, 1954. Above the front spare track link on the sponson is an armored first-aid kit. Often these kits were mounted at an angle on the sponson, but this one is mounted parallel to the fender. *National Archives*

Members of the 60th Ordnance Group, I US Corps, use an M62 wrecker to install a 76 mm gun with a new barrel in an M4A3(76) W with HVSS at the base of the 8th Republic of Korea (ROK) Army Tank Battalion, on December 27, 1954. This tank evidently is one that was transferred to the ROK army during or just after the Korean War. Another M4A3(76)W with HVSS is in the center background, with a tarpaulin over the turret. *National Archives*